I0704420

We Ugly Humans

ISBN: 9798655504394
Library of Congress Control Number: 2020912692
Independently Published
North Charleston, South Carolina, USA

To all the eristic I know

Other Titles by

Andrew S. S. Chan

The Invisible Rings: A Long-distant Love Story
At the Tea House: Where D.S. meets B.S.
Are We Lucky or What
Common Sense for Good Health & Longevity
Mu Mo: The Accidental Monk Golfer
Hooker Daughter Beggar Father

Paperback and E-book are available at Amazon.com, Barnes and Noble, or at any other major bookstores.

Acknowledgement

Introduction: The Debate

The debate, hosted by a major TV network, was held and televised on a Saturday evening in Los Angeles. It was an impressive event with thirteen luminary guests: two veteran political commentators, a navy general, two professors from elite universities, a former attorney general, a Republican ex-governor, a Democratic former congresswoman, one social activist, one social worker, a policeman, an environmentalist, and the author of a controversial book, *We Ugly Humans*, on which the topics of the debate was based. Although the book was published only recently, it had already caused quite a disturbance in the social and political circles of this country, if not of the whole world, because the author, Mr. Lee, not afraid of offending anyone, had courageously and honestly confronted head-on the problems we are having today.

Almost like a business conference, the format of the debate and the seating arrangement was very casual: the debate host occupied the head of a long conference table and the author the end of it, and the other twelve debaters were seated on both sides. The debate host, doubled as a moderator and a fireman, had determined to leave his guests alone so that they could debate freely – from their hearts instead of from their brains. Only when the debate should get too personal would he come in to put out the fire with his fire extinguisher.

The purpose of the debate was to gather some of the best brains in the country to discuss those problems mentioned in Mr. Lee's book more comprehensively and, hopefully, through the brainstorming meeting they might come up with some sensible solutions.

List of Debate Panelists

The debate host: Mr. Medford

He is a veteran journalist, a celebrated TV personality and the anchorman of the Evening News for the past sixteen years. He is a gregarious and diplomatically affable man. What I mean is that he may not be affable at times; all depends on his state of mood. He has an air that exudes confidence and authority, but he is a fair man though, and he has made a name for himself out of it. As a debate host his credential is impeccable. Besides having interviewed with many important people around the world, he has hosted more than anyone else in history presidential campaign debates.

The author: Mr. Lee

He is a lean old man of eighty years old but he looks like he is in his late sixty. He went to the debate wearing exactly the same outfit that he had worn on his wedding day fifty-something years ago, not just the dark gray suit but also the skinny navy-blue tie, the white shirt, and the black shoes and socks. He had saved the ensemble for important occasions, and he considered this debate was one of them besides his children's and grandchildren's weddings. But, because he had been shrinking a bit over the decades, the white shirt and the dark gray suit no longer fit him perfectly; they were too long and too loose and not to mention they were way out of fashion. Nobody at the meeting had met him before but they paid him undue attentions when he first entered the room, for he looked more like an idle thinker from the eighteen century than a modern day writer.

He stumbled into this televised debate by accident because of his highly controversial book which had won several major awards and was on the best-seller list for seven consecutive weeks. And, because it is about our current political and social ills, which are red-hot debate topics these days, he was invited to participate in a debate with twelve other well-known people from different backgrounds. He has never been in a debate before, in fact; he has never involved in a heated argument with friends. But he is an excellent analyst who can tell, at the blink of his eyes, the rights and wrongs of an argument. He is a quick thinker too; his brain works faster than a super computer. He was born a debater and he doesn't know it. When he was first invited to the debate, he turned it down flat to the astonishment of Mr. Medford whose invitations has never yet been declined. He not only had doubts in his ability to argue convincingly in public, under the lime lights of cameras and before so many strangers, but also worried about his lack of debate experience. Debating with such a large group of experts might prove to be too intimidating. But after having learned that the debate would be confined only to the topics in his book, which to him were as familiar as the back of his hands, his confidence restored and he thought: if I can argue in my book, I should be able to argue with anyone. Finally, with the urgings from his publisher who foresaw a big jump in sales of his book after the debate, he reluctantly agreed to give it a try.

The right-leaning commentator: Mr. Rosenthal
He is a typical conservative Republican and has been an advisor to two Republican presidents. As an advocate of capitalism and traditionalism, he objects to all

forms of changes and doesn't believe in welfare. And because he was growing up poor and had been working his way up all by himself through hard work and dedication, he has little sympathy for beggars and lazybones. He always says: if they are able to beg they should be able to work too!

The left-leaning commentator: Mrs. Smith

She makes her mark by being a shrewd debater; she knows how to double down or to back down, so that she is always on the winning side no matter what, and without offending anyone.

The navy general: Mr. Frost

The General is an out-spoken man, very unusual for a sailor, but he speaks like a sailor though – from his heart and not from his brain – blunt and crude and, more often than not, offensive to the person he speaks to.

The Democratic former congresswoman: Mrs. Faith

She, a trial lawyer, got famous for representing quite a few celebrity women in high-profiled sexual harassment lawsuits. Her aggressive style of liberalism had won her a one-termed seat in Congress.

The Republican Ex-governor: Mr. Rosen

He and his family are professional politicians. His grandfather and father were governors before him and, now, his two sons are holding public offices – one is a state senator and the other, a district attorney – with an ambition to succeed him. He is an effective governor though, during his reign his state was among the most prosperous in the country.

The former attorney general: Mr. Hill

He is more of a law professor than of a politician, for he doesn't know how to play politics but knows all the technicalities of the law and the U.S. Constitution. He had earned high marks when he was in office and he is still well-respected.

The liberal professor: Mrs. Chow

Mrs. Chow teaches Asian Study at a prestigious university which is well-known for its liberal policies of promoting diversity, trying to create a harmonious melting pot. It has more ethnic studies and ethnic associations than the number of nations in the world and, despite its noble intent of uniting the divided world, it actually further divides it. Mrs. Chow, an Irish-American, changed her last name to Chow after marrying her eager Chinese teacher while she was an exchange student studying Chinese history in China. Her knowledge of Chinese culture is limited at best, let alone other Asian cultures. How she got her teaching job with an elite college is a mystery.

The conservative professor: Dr. Cain

Dr. Cain, on the contrary, has distinguished credentials; he has a Ph.D. in American history from an elite university where he has been teaching for the past twenty years. He is a typical historian, apolitical and honest, and he always sticks to verifiable facts.

The social activist: Miss Jones

She is an antagonistic and adamant social activist from Chicago. Her fierce and unyielding style in the fight for social justice has made her a hero among her people. But her success turned her into an extremist.

The social worker: Mr. Brown

His full-time job is a social worker but his part-time job is a civil right activist. His Southern root makes him an opposite of Miss Jones; he is soft-spoken, polite, and compromising, but he is not without ambition though; he aims to be the first black president and often compares himself with the late Dr. King.

The environmentalist: Dr. Davis

He has impressive credentials too; he has a Ph.D. in environmental biology and a MBA. He had a two-year stint with Peace Corp and has been working for United Nation as an environmental researcher for the past three years.

The policeman: Mr. Hernandez

He is a veteran, big city policeman with twenty years of experience to his credit. He was invited to the debate merely because he is a Mexican-American police-man working in Hispanic community.

Chapter 1: Discrimination

Immediately after he finished introducing all his guests and made sure they were all seated, the debate host, Mr. Medford, picked up a book in front of him and said as he was holding it up above his head.

Mr. Medford: I'm sure you all have read the book I sent you. Isn't it a very interesting book? It covers a lot of important subjects that we are facing today, most of them are problematic. I must say, Mr. Lee has done a good job with it. His honest and bold opinions and refreshing ideas may be a bit controversial, but I think they are quite stimulating. Stimulation is what we need these days, to find new ideas and new approaches to solve the persistent problems that we have. That's why we are here today, to be stimulated, to be bold, to be honest with ourselves, to be free to speak out our feelings without having to worry about offending anyone or be offended.

Ladies and Gentlemen, I want to remind you, please limit your discussions within the scope of Mr. Lee's book. I'm sure we all have some agreements and disagreements with Mr. Lee or with each other, but we should keep an open mind and listen to what others have to say first. Most importantly, we're all friends here, trying to brainstorm out some solutions to our problems; so, no matter how intense our arguments are, please don't let us lose our civility. Now, who is going to start first?

Many raised their hands but Mr. Medford picked Mrs. Smith, not for any particular reason other than that she happened to be sitting in front of him.

Mrs. Smith: Mr. Lee, in your book you said, "Discrimination is everywhere; not only we, humans, have it, all animals, birds, fish and even insects have it. We had it in the past and we have it now and we'll have it in the future." If what you said is true, why should we spend the time and energy fighting against it? Don't you agree we have made tremendous progress in this area? I choose "discrimination" first because I think it is the single most troublesome problem we have right now. It is so divisive and damaging. If we can solve this problem first, I think we can solve many other problems later.

Mr. Lee: Absolutely, we've made great progress, but at the expense of more divisiveness and hostility.

Mrs. Smith: It can't be. We've tried our best to make people aware of the problem and to educate them that bigotry is a social ill and it has no place in our modern society.

Mr. Lee: That's the problem. We have magnified the problem to the point that we actually make it worse. We overcook it, so to speak, with racial and sexual discriminations leading the way. There are many other different kinds of discriminations and some of them are not even discriminations at all. The word "discrimination" by definition is the treatment or consideration of, or making a distinction in favor of or against, a person or thing based on the group, class, or category to which that person or thing belongs rather than on individual merit. So, if the action, either favorable or unfavorable, is based on individual merit, then it is not discrimination. Many of us fail to make the distinction and thus use the word incorrectly and loosely. Minorities, women, disables, gays and lesbians and transgender often claim they are being discriminated against when they couldn't get in the college of their choice, when they're passed over for a promotion, when they get lousy service from a lousy waitress, or when they're being looked at a second too long. In short, we use the word "discrimination" so loosely that we often use it as an excuse to justify our groundless complains or to cover up the truths or to simply get attentions. Police pursuit is a good example; the more and longer the pursuits are shown on TV, the more pursuits we're going to have. Do you know why? There are a lot of crazy people out there; they think it is fun, exciting, and glamour to be chased by a dozen of police cruisers with their colorful lights flashing for hours from freeway to freeway, and they are very proud of their mischiefs because in the eyes of their peers they are instant heroes.

Miss Jones: Are you implying those people who claim being discriminated against are attention-getters too?

Mr. Lee: No, Miss Jones. I meant media brings too much attention to discrimination cases that it encourages some of us use the word "discrimination" way too freely. Oh, let me give you another example which I think is clearer than police pursuit. I grew up in a small village way out in the country, we children were very much afraid of ghosts because villagers were telling ghost stores all the time. After dark we were afraid to go into a room alone in our own house. Our children grew up in the city and they seldom heard people talking about ghosts, so they were never afraid of the dark and hardly knew what a ghost is. Any psychologist can tell you, if a rumor is repeated often and spread wide enough, it will become believable. That is how brainwash and propaganda work. I think we should, before we make a claim of discrimination, find out whether we are really discriminated and, if we are, what kind of discrimination it is. More importantly, we should

put away our self-deceiving pride and do a little self-examination and ask ourselves this question: why are we not liked? If we are not liked because it is our own fault, such as: either because we are talking too loud, using too much profanity, dressing distastefully, acting like a jerk, or simply having an inferiority complex, then, it isn't discrimination. But, if we are not liked because the color of our skin, nationality, gender, age, deformity, or all other things that are not our own fault, then, it is discrimination. Discrimination comes in many forms; even poor people would discriminate rich people because they think all rich people are snobbish and would look down on them. Also, discrimination can be favorable too, for example, we discriminate beggars because we think all beggars are poor and need help and, therefore, we tend to show some kindness and give them some money. Discrimination is a rather confusing word, no wonder so many people get it all wrong. We have to be careful with it and should examine it case by case before we yell, "I'm discriminated!"
Miss Jones: Why people have to discriminate, we're all human beings?
Mr. Lee: Just because we're humans. You see, we humans are born with so many flaws. Nobody is perfect. All of us have some good natures and some bad natures. People who discriminate are those who let their bad natures take control of them.

Long before Mr. Lee finished answering her question; Miss Jones had already got lost by his elaborate explanations of good and bad human natures, although they were perfectly clear to everyone else. But she was that kind of a person who is too proud to admit but to blame everything on others.

Chapter 2: Racial Discrimination

Miss Jones: You've confused the hack out of me for sure. You don't like someone because he, for example, has bad breaths isn't racial discrimination?

Mr. Lee: Yes or no, it all depends on the particular situation. Now, how can I make it clearer for you? Okay. It is discrimination if I dislike all the people with bad breaths regardless of their races. But, it is racial discrimination if I don't dislike all the people with bad breaths but only those of certain race. Is it clear to you, Miss Jones?

Miss Jones: You don't like his bad breaths but you can still like him as a person, can't you?

Mr. Lee: Yes, I can but I have to keep ten feet away from him. I have some friends who have bad breaths once in a while. I don't like their bad breaths but I still like them. Generally, I don't like people have bad breaths and that is discrimination.

Miss Jones: So, it is racial discrimination if that someone happens to be a colored person. Am I right?

Mr. Lee: Not necessarily. Unless the reason you don't like that person is also based on race.

Miss Jones: Then, how can I know what your dislike is based on? You can tell me anything you want to, right?

Mr. Lee: Pretty much so.

Miss Jones: If that's the case, bigots can get away with discriminatory acts easily and that's not right!

Mr. Lee: I'm afraid they can if they choose to camouflage their prejudices, but most likely they don't. You see, bigots are people who think they are more superior and better, and they get their satisfactions from showing their contempt and seeing their victims suffer. More often than

not they are ignorant people and they either don't want to or don't have the sophistications to hide their distasteful acts.
Miss Jones: As far as I'm concerned, anyone who dislikes minorities is a racist.

Though old and lean Mr. Lee still has a lot of fire, and his temper is still as hot as the Chinese red pepper he has been eating daily. He was getting a little annoyed by the activist's arbitrary but insistent arguments.

Mr. Lee: Let me ask you a question if I may, Miss Jones. If you come onto a bus and sit next to me and your breaths smell bad, so I move away and sit somewhere else. What do you think of me?
Miss Jones: You're a racist!
Mr. Lee: No, I'm not. I get away from you because of your bad breaths only, not because the color of your skin.
Miss Jones: What's the difference? You exhibit hatred and prejudice toward me and that is racism.
Mr. Lee: There's a huge difference. I don't hate you, in fact, I like you a lot because you're a charming person, and I don't hate your race either, so, my discriminatory reaction can't be racial. I hate people with bad breaths, period, not just you, but all the people with bad breaths regardless what races they belong. You may call this kind of discrimination "Discrimination of bad-breath-people," but definitely you can't call it racial discrimination.
Miss Jones: I still don't get it. Can't you speak more clearly? You have a funny accent, you know.
Mr. Lee: Okay, let me put it differently. Suppose that person is not me but a black man, do you still call him a racist?

Miss Jones: Uh—Uh, yes! It doesn't matter if he is White, Yellow, Brown, Red, or Black.

Mr. Lee: He can't be a racist! How can one racially discriminate one's own people? His moving away from you is an indication that he either dislikes people with bad breaths or you as a person. You see, Miss Jones, so many people like you use "racial discrimination" for all kinds of discrimination because they either have an inferiority complex or being ignorant.

Miss Jones, a dedicated activist from Chicago, who has been staunchly fighting racism for years, but the longer she has fought, the more she hates other races, and she has become a racist herself without knowing it. She had been practically shut up by Mr. Lee's sarcastic last remark which had touched her sensitive nerve. She couldn't find anything to shoot back but sitting there with her face turning red and puffing air like a fuming toad. Mr. Medford, the debate host doubled as a fireman, saw the fire was coming and he rushed in with a fire extinguisher, just in case the fire should break out.

Mr. Medford: Since we've got into racial discrimination which is a major issue these days, we may as well talk a little more about it. Mr. Lee, do you mind explaining to us why you think the term "racial discrimination" has been grossly misused?

Mr. Lee: Just a few minutes ago, an intelligent person like Miss Jones has misused it; you can imagine how many more not-so-intelligent people would have done the same. The underlining reason is: America is a big melting pot; we have so many races with different cultures. Aside from the first wave of immigrants who came to America as explorers and conquerors (mostly Whites), later waves of immigrants were slaves, refugees, or poor laborers (mostly Blacks and Browns). And because they, as a group or a race, were poor and had low social status, they were routinely abused and discriminated against by the White folks, who came to this country first. After generations of put down and looked down, they felt they were second-class citizens, which still haunts them today even when they are free and being treated equally. Another reason is that the young generations of the White majority now realize that their ancestors had been wrong the way they'd treated the slaves and other minorities, they feel they have the need to making up for them. And because of this they embolden some minorities to take advantage of their guilty consciences and use racial discrimination as a winning excuse.

The embarrassment had long gone out of Miss Jones by now, but not her anger; she is known to be an adamant fighter and she wouldn't let a little setback to disarm her easily. So she asked Mr. Lee in an authoritative tone.

Miss Jones: So there are no real racial discriminations, they are all imaginations dreamed up by attention-getting minorities in order to gain some sympathies from White folks, right?

Though not very pleased, Mr. Lee didn't want to force the debate host to bring out the fire extinguisher again, and also, he suddenly remembered what his father had once warned him, "Son, never fight with a woman, you'll never win." So, he said as calmly and tactfully as he possibly could and added a little smile here and there, as if he had already forgotten their previous bitterness.

Mr. Lee: I wouldn't say that, Miss Jones. No question about it racism exists; some of us do discriminate others because of their race. Usually, racists are those who live all their lives in a small world of their own and seldom have the opportunity to interact with other people besides their own race. They are not necessarily bigots; they simply don't know anything better, for they form their opinions about other races based on the information from media and other unreliable sources, and not from their own experiences of dealing directly with people of other races. It doesn't mean smart and educated people can't be racists. People become racists for so many different reasons: they can be inherently bad people who hate the whole world or can be angry people who suffer from multitudes of things or have had an unpleasant experience with a certain race. Whatever their reasons are, we should never react with hostility. We should feel sorry for them and ignore them and that is all we can do. You see, racism is all in our heads; if we *think* it is then it is, or, if we think it isn't then it isn't. Therefore, we shouldn't use racism as a shield to defend our own faults as so many people do nowadays. They blame racism for setting them back in education or career without admitting that they are lazy and unmotivated. They accuse the not-so-friendly waiters and the forceful policemen as racists. But they never ask themselves why they behave so negatively in a restaurant and why they verbally abuse police officers and resist arrests with violence.

Once I went to a friend's party and for no apparent reason we got into the topic of racial discrimination. One friend said that the state of Alabama was the worst in the country; the waiters were rude and the gas station attendants inattentive. I asked him if they were all Whites, and he said, "No! Some of them were Blacks." You see, my friend had arbitrarily made the assumption that the ill-treatments he received were the result of racial discrimination. The truth is that it may not be the case; it could be something else, such as: they were unhappy people or my friend didn't treat them right. We have no way to know for sure because it depends on what those presumed racists thought of my friend at the time. If they thought of him as a Chinese, which they didn't like, even though he'd done nothing to offend them, then it is racism. If they thought of him as a nasty person only, then, it isn't.

Actually, racial discrimination is very rare these days; it has improved a lot since those days when minorities were not allowed to use White restrooms, ride White buses, and dine at White restaurants; and they did not have voting rights and their children couldn't go to White schools. Everything was segregated. Now, they can do all these things. So many members of minorities nowadays are being treated as if they were royalties and people would roll out red carpets for them. On the other hand, some poor Whites are being treated like trashes, not only by their own people but also by other minorities as well. In general, if you're rich or famous or nice to others, you are respected and welcome, and if you're poor or having a disagreeable personality, you are denigrated. This isn't *racial* discrimination; it's *class* discrimination – the *haves* against the *have-nots,* and the *nice* against the *nasty*. And no laws can ever change that.

Miss Jones: Since we're all born equal there is no reason why poor people should be discriminated. They aren't all bad and rich and famous people aren't all good either. Why should we look down the poor and look up the rich and famous?

Mr. Lee: I agree with you totally, Miss Jones, and I wish we don't. But, unfortunately, it's one of the human natures that we are born with: to put down people below us and worship those above us, and there is nothing we can do about it unless we change our attitudes through learning. Some of us can learn but some of us can't. I wrote in my book that we had discrimination before and we have it today and we'll have it in the future. So, discrimination will be here to stay. It is just too bad that not all of us can change the human natures that we are born with.

Miss Jones: What human natures you're talking about?

Mr. Lee: There are many, some are good and some are bad. The good ones are: unselfishness, generosity, sacrifice, bravery, empathy, and, of course, love, and so on. The bad ones are: greed, selfishness, hatred, aggression, envy, vanity, jealousy, self-pity, prejudice, possessiveness, and so on. We acquire most of the human natures at birth but later, through learnings or under the influence of our environments we might be able to change, for better or for worse, some of them.

Miss Jones got more confused by the bombardment of so many different human natures that she finally gave up trying to understand.

Miss Jones: May I ask you a personal question, Mr. Lee?

Mr. Lee: Sure, you may.

Miss Jones: Have you any friends?

Mr. Lee: Of course, I have friends.

Miss Jones: I mean African-American friends.

Mr. Lee was surprised that Miss Jones would ask such a question which was completely unrelated to what they were discussing. He hesitated, tapping his head for a while, but managed to regain his composure shortly.

Mr. Lee: No, I have none. I know a few nice fellows though, but they aren't close enough that I'd call them friends.
Miss Jones: What are the races of your friends?
Mr. Lee: Well, I don't have that many friends, only a few old friends. Let me think, three Whites, two Koreans, one Mexican, and a half dozen or so Chinese.
Miss Jones: Are they all males?
Mr. Lee: Yes. It's very dangerous to have girlfriends these days, you know, especially at my age.

Mr. Lee was very unhappy with all these silly questions; he began to suspect what the activist was driving at. But, he managed to camouflage his annoyance and apprehension by throwing in a joke which aroused a roaring laugher.

Miss Jones: Only one Hispanic, no African American and no female, you must be a racist and a sexist, then.

The unwarranted accusation had killed the roaring laughter instantly, turning merry round faces into melancholy long faces. Nobody could believe she would have used such offensive words to attack a fine gentleman like Mr. Lee. They waited nervously for his response.

Mr. Lee: What! You call me a racist and a sexist just because I have none of your race and your gender as a friend? Young lady, let me tell you something, if I ever should become a racist and a sexist, it is because of *you*!

Mr. Lee shouted, standing up to face the activist and letting his hot temper explode as freely as if he were at home and forgetting he was in a civil debate with a dozen of important people. This unexpected incident caught everyone off-guard, including Mr. Lee himself. He was so embarrassed by his own out-of-control quick temper that he forgot to sit down, not until the debate host signaled him to do so. As to Miss Jones, she was so shock by Mr. Lee's rage that she nearly fainted. She sat there, dazed, like a statute in a museum, undecided what to do next. All of a sudden, the conference room was so quiet, like a museum with fourteen statuses looking at one another, pondering for the future.

Mr. Medford: Miss Jones, please don't use such a strong language. Mr. Lee is much older than us and should be respected. Now, let's continue our discussion. I think we can improve racial relationship by discouraging segregation. If all races have more contacts and interactions with one another, we'll know one another better and eventually eliminate a lot of misunderstandings among us. What do you think, Mr. Lee?

Mr. Lee: Well—well, sure—sure it will help. But knowing each other well doesn't eliminate discrimination or prejudice completely; it may improve on racial discrimination but not on other forms of discriminations. We don't have to look far, just look at our own family, among our siblings. Do we not know each other well? But some of us are our parents' favorites and some aren't; some are the favorites of our fathers but not of our mothers, or vice versa; and we all get different treatments accordingly. You may wonder why, we're all raised by the same parents and eat the same food. The reason is that we aren't born equal; some of us are smarter, healthier and behave better than the others. Parents too, their preferences aren't the same either; they may like boys better than girls or the other way around, and they may be more sympathetic with the sick and the weak, and thus treat them more tenderly. Although it's not *discrimination*, but it's unquestionably bias. If a small family is already like this, you can imagine what it is like for a society, for a country, and for the world. So, knowing each other well doesn't necessarily make us less discriminatory, but at least it should help us to tolerate each other better and thus enable us to make the necessary adjustments and compromises easier.

The solution shouldn't be governmental mandates or more new laws, which in my opinion are *divisive* rather than *unifying*. Just take a look at the many different languages we use in letters and forms our government agencies sending out to us – English, Chinese, Hindi, Spanish, Arabic, Japanese, and even Russian – and the words we use to describe who we are: African-American, Chinese-American, Native-American, and so on. Africa has 54 countries, which one of those that an African-American belongs to? And, Native-Americans might not be the first inhabitants living in America. I am classified as a Chinese-American and I don't know I belong to People's Republic of China, Republic of China, or Hong Kong. All I know is that my ancestors are Chinese and I'm an American citizen now. I travel with an American passport and I pay my taxes to United States. Come on, we are all Americans; this is our home and our future. Does it matter from where we or our ancestors originally came from?

Another divisive element is our leaders. They are so divided along party line, racial line, nationality line, and religious line that they can't work together; instead, they fight with one another to protect their own interests. Leaders should set a good example for their citizens just like parents for their children. They should put aside their personal differences and interests and be able to work together for common good. This country is supposed to be a great melting pot where different races and different nationalities with different cultures mix together and learn from one another to make this a great country for all of us. But instead, each race isolates themselves within their own walls – China Town, Korean Town, Little Tokyo, Little Saigon, Mexican Town, and Jews District, etc. – They have their own area and speak their own language as if they were still living in their old country. As a result, what we get is not a delicious dish but a tasteless, troublesome smorgasbord.

Taking recent protest as an example, you can see how divided our country is. Protesters are blocking the streets and freeways, burning properties and looting stores. No doubt about it, the police does have a problem that needs to be addressed and changed. There are too many racist cops who routinely use excessive force toward minorities. The offenders and collaborators should be brought to justice and punished for their crimes, and we have all the rights to make our voice heard and force for a change in police culture and policy. But, most cops are good cops and shouldn't be treated as our enemies. Treating police as a bad guy is the same as assuming all policemen are bad, and that's discrimination itself. Also, violent protest hurts so many innocent people, who are commuters, truck drivers, store owners, and they are our neighbors and friends, and they can be White, Black, Brown, Yellow, and Red. Especially during this time when we are facing the worst pandemic crisis in history, prolonged violent protest with millions of people packed together without wearing any mask, not only makes our already bad economy worse, but also makes controlling the spread of the virus much more difficult. Who is paying for the loss of livelihoods and lives? Of course, it's we, the common people! Think about it, protesters are supposed to fight for justice for the victims of police brutality, but, due to emotionally thoughtlessness, their extreme actions end up creating a lot more victims. Victims are victims, lives are lives and they are *all* matter! Not just Black lives! Black Lives Matter movement itself is very racist.

I really think it is wrong for us minorities to assume all White people are racists and our enemies. Sure, they have some bad people, so have we. But, most White folks are good people and they treat us as we are their equals. If we're totally honest with ourselves, we can't deny we, one time or the other, have a White folk helping us and treating us as a friend. It is grossly unfair and ungrateful to group them with a small percentage of insensitive White bigots. If you want my opinion, Black Live Matter movement doesn't represent the majority of Black folks; it is organized by a few hateful, self-serving power grabbers who, instead of improving equality and racism, stir up resentments among races and disfranchise the supports of the majority White. In the end it will further divide us along racial lines and thus hurt not just the Whites, but also all minorities.

Miss Jones had been very quiet and unhappy after Mr. Medford's intervention, and she was shaking her head continuously when Mr. Lee was speaking; evidently she disagreed with everything he said.

Miss Jones: I don't see adding a word "Black" to "All Lives Matter" is racist. Our people suffer from racism the most, more than any race. Do you know, Mr. Lee, that the chance for a Black man getting incarcerated or killed is disproportionally high?

Mr. Lee: Of course I know. I bet you don't know why.

Miss Jones: Why, of course it's racism! What else?

Mr. Lee: No. The number of Black people killed by their own people is disproportional, too, a lot more than by the White. Let me tell you why: it is because there are more gangs, more crimes, and more violence in the Black community.

Miss Jones: We people commit more crimes because we're poor, and we resist arrest because we're afraid of going to jail which is a horrible place where they torture and beat us like we're animals.

Mr. Lee: I have nothing against Black people but I have plenty against their leaders and the hypocritical White sympathizers and the copycats of other minorities. They use racism and inequality to empower themselves and to enrich their own wallets. How? First, they sow hatred to stir up unrest and hostility among the people, and then they organize protests and fund-raisings, all for selfish reasons. What they should be doing is to address the problems honestly and fairly, telling their people to learn from other minorities who are thriving in this country and seldom have problems with the law, motivating them to work hard and be successful. The White folks too, their attitudes toward minorities should be changed. We're not living in the past when the White majority was slave master. We are all equal now and nobody is better than the others. Only when we all realize that we must change our attitudes, respecting each other's rights that we can truly achieve equality and live in harmony.

However, solving racial discrimination problems should be done by us, ourselves, individually, and voluntarily, not by protesting and destroying properties and lootings and demanding. We must make an effort to improve ourselves as a person (getting rid of our faulty human natures), to ignore our differences (whatever our differences are), and try to accept the fact that there always *will be* discrimination and prejudice in this world. Life is not perfect, the world is not perfect, and we humans are not perfect, so don't expect ideal. This is so easy for me because I listen to my father's advice: if people don't like you, don't complain but ask yourself why and how can you make them like you. When I first came to this country, I met a lot of people who liked me and also quite a few disliked me. You know what? By following my father's advice, I not only made some of the people didn't like me before my friends but, more importantly, I never ever felt the effect of the *ugly* word, "racism."

Mr. Lee's emotional speech ended in exceedingly loud voice, which rendered everyone in the room speechless. They all wondered why they had never thought of these things before.

Chapter 3: Sexual Discrimination

Mrs. Chow: After reading your book in which you said sexual discrimination is like racial discrimination: over claimed, especially after the so-called #MeToo movement, I got the feeling that you're not very sympathetic to us women who are fighting every day for survival in a male-dominating world.

Mr. Lee: I'm sorry you feel that way, Mrs. Chow, #MeToo is a good movement to begin with; it brings the much needed attention to inequality, abuse, and other forms of ill-treatments that many females in the world are suffering from. But not all females are mistreated and not all males are misogynists. However, I am sure there are some males, who are either bad people or uncivilized like other animals, mistreat females. But, most of us civilized males treat females fairly and respectfully. Because females are generally built smaller and weaker in strength, we males end up doing all the heavy and demanding works, such as farming, hunting and fishing, and leaving the house and office works for females, which are lighter and less dangerous. And, we males are not necessarily the bosses in the house, who make all the important decisions. A lot of times the females are. Through the influence of pillow-talks, many powerful females in history ran the country through their husbands. By the way, how can we discriminate and mistreat the very people we love: our mothers, wives, and daughters who are undoubtedly the dearest persons in our life? I have to admit that there are many Asians and Arabians who are still sticking to their old traditions that favor males more than females, and that needs to be changed. But females in the Western world are treated, in my opinion, rather too civilly. We open the doors for them, we pull back the chairs for them to sit, and in so many ways we treat them like they were babies. So, sexual discrimination goes both ways – favorable and unfavorable.

Mrs. Chow: But we can't deny that there are a lot of sexual harassments and abuses going on though. It has become a serious problem and we can't ignore it anymore, can we?"

Mr. Lee: Again, there is no question about it that some of us males sexually abuse and harass females, but they are bad and insensitive males who have not yet learned how to control their natural instincts. Humans are animals too, no different from other animals; males are born aggressive and dominating because they are usually bigger and stronger. Take a look at other animals like dogs, lions, monkeys, bulls, and even elephants; it is the males who assume the roles as protectors of their families, defending them from encroaching enemies, it is the males who fight for a mate, and it is the males who initiate the romance of mating. Their behaviors are natural and inborn and so are ours. So, what is wrong for a man to look at a woman with desire and ask her for a date? None! However, since we are civilized animals and have developed a code of decency through years of experiences and necessities, it is highly inappropriate for a man to follow a woman around and sniff her rear end or expose himself like other animals do (for we wear clothes and other animals don't). Unfortunately, there are always some uncivilized men in this world who cannot control their animalistic desires and, therefore, behave inappropriately.

Mrs. Chow: So we need #MeToo movement. It raises public awareness of the problem and encourages women to come out to expose the offenders. We women have been keeping quiet for so long that we are kind of accepting abuses and harassments as something normal. I think it is about time to change all these.

Mr. Lee: I agree. The #MeToo movement may offer some hopes to stop the regressions of some men. But the problem is that the movement was started by a bunch of very liberal women who are, for various reasons, very hateful of men. The silent majority is traditional women and they don't want to change things drastically; instead, they use love and compassion to work on a gradual change. Now, any woman can destroy not only a man's reputation and his career but also his family by simply opening her mouth, accusing a man of sexual harassment or abuse, which, if it is true had happened a long time ago; and she can do it without any proof and her word is the verdict, and she doesn't have to be held accountable either. A man may get fired from his job because his company or organization wants to distant itself from him, lest it will be accused for protecting him, and also, he may get divorced by his jealous wife who believes the scandal more than her husband.

According to our law, one is innocent until proven guilty. Now, a man is guilty and ruined by a few one-sided words from a woman. Where is the justice? Don't we need to hear from the man, too? Don't we need proof? Don't we need to check into the accuser's credibility? Why didn't she say something at the time when it happened? Don't we need to find out the accuser is just as guilty as the accused by giving him the opportunity? Don't we need to know what kind of character she is? More importantly, don't we need to ask her what her motive is to speak out now instead of before? Before we

have the answers for all these questions, it's wrong to de-
clare a man guilty as charged and punish him for it.

Mrs. Chow: As a woman myself I do think #MeToo is a
bit one-sided. We have bad women among us too; not all
women are good and innocent. I personally know one bad
one who is aspired to be an actress. When she fails to get
the part in a movie after she has sold her body and soul to
a producer, she accuses the producer of rape, and that was
more than ten years ago. I am not sure her accusation is
groundless or the accused is innocent; I just want to make
sure the accused gets a fair trial and the accuser punished
if she makes a false accusation. That's only fair.

Mr. Lee: I think it is very fair; an innocent man deserves
protection as much as an innocent woman.

Mrs. Faith: I believe in most cases the accused are guilty
as charged. Men have been abusing women for a long
time, especially in the entertainment industry because
they hold the power of "make or break" a career, and
there are many eager preys. But, before the #MeToo not
many women dare to expose the offenders because of the
potential embarrassment and humiliation to testify in
court, and I think they are also ashamed of their own na-
ivety and eagerness. Especially true for domestic violence
and abuse; women rather prefer to tolerate and suffer than
making it open, for they are afraid of getting devoiced and
their children ruined.

Mr. Lee: You are absolutely right, Mrs. Faith, the same
thing is true, too, for men. You'll be surprised how many
men are the victims of domestic violence and abuse. A
lot! Most yelling and dish-throwing are done by women,
not men, and they abuse their husbands by boycotting
cooking for them and by depriving them of sex. Can men
open up on this sort of thing? Absolutely not! They can't

even disclose it to their best friends like women do. Yes, some men are brutal and abusive, but some are nice and tame like lambs, and I know some of them like that.

Mrs. Faith: I wonder why you're telling us this now, are you one of them?

Mrs. Faith's wisecrack got the whole room smiling with the exception of Miss Jones and Mr. Hernandez. In the former's eye Mr. Lee was still an old-fashioned racist and sexist, and his talk of female abusers was a disguised way to attack women. But to the later it was all too real; he had seen it many times before when he was dispatched to the scene of domestic fights.

Mr. Hernandez: What Mr. Lee said is true. I've seen it all the time with my own two eyes over all these years as a policeman. So often I saw the house was in a mess and the woman was still cussing and yelling while her poor husband was cowering embarrassingly in a corner, where broken glass, chinaware, magazines, and whatever were all over the place around him. My partner got hit once by a flying dish and I had a near miss twice.

Miss Jones: So, what's a big deal throwing a few dishes when her man beats her up, uh? A real woman got to fight back! Anyway, it isn't the same when you compare to women getting raped and broken bones! Haven't you seen any black-eyed and nose-bleeding women on duty, Mr. Hernandez?

Mr. Hernandez: I've seen some.

Mr. Lee was quietly furious, he had had enough of Miss Jones's preposterous arguments, and he intended to teach her once more a lesson. But, he had to find a way to do it in such a way that the debate host, Mr. Medford, wouldn't have to take out his fire extinguisher again.

Mr. Lee: Men can get broken bones too if the woman is strong enough, fortunately, men cannot be raped, I'm sure you know why, Miss Jones. But, they can be seduced by women, and they do, naturally, all the time. Who can resist a charming lady showing off her best form before your eye? In my opinion rape and seduction is the same thing. There is law to punish a man for rape but no law to punish a woman for seduction, how unfair!
Miss Jones: I don't know why you're so hateful of women. Have you been seduced?
Mr. Lee: No. I'm too old and unattractive. Maybe you want to try?

This time, Mr. Lee's jest was a great disappointment; nobody laughed. They all thought he went way too far, and he knew that, too, after had noticed Mr. Medford's reproving glance. In order to salvage the awkward situation without giving Miss Jones an apology, which he thought unnecessary, he turned to Mr. Medford and asked if he could continue to the other forms of discriminations. Under this awkward situation, Mr. Medford, was quick and happy to grant him the permission.

Chapter 4: Discrimination of Disabled Person

Mr. Lee: There is a discrimination which I think is the cruelest, and that's the discrimination against disabled people. They are easy victims, unable to fight back due to their disabilities which are born with or acquired later through injuries or diseases. We discriminate them for something not even their fault. They are victims of misfortune of which they have no control. So, we should show a little compassion by helping them instead of discriminating them.

Mrs. Faith: We do. We'd passed the Disability Act which benefits the disables in so many different ways, to make their lives less miserable. I can say that much, our disables are the luckiest in the world. I've travelled to many parts of the world and have seen many disables; they are dirty and sick-looking and begging in the streets. They live like unwanted animals.

Mr. Frost: I must say that Disability Act and modern technology have helped many disabled veterans. Many public facilities and businesses now have handicap accesses and parking spaces dedicated to them, which make it much easier for them to conduct their daily activities, subsequently, they are healthier and happier.

Dr. Cain: More importantly, thanks to the Disability Act which enables them to get better psychological and physical therapies. With artificial limbs they can move around like a normal person and don't have to sit in the wheelchair all day long, rotting. Now, they are more active and can participate in many sports. They even have their own Olympics, and through competitions they regain their self-esteems and happiness.

Mr. Hernandez: I'm glad our government finally realizes handicaps are people too. According to some of my former colleagues who are disables now because of the injuries they had incurred on the job, that they can find another job much easier now because of the artificial legs and arms.

Chapter 5: Discrimination of LGTBQ

Mrs. Faith: I have a question to ask you, Mr. Lee. In your book, you have much sympathy for disabled people, but very little for LGTBQ. I wonder why?

Mr. Lee: Maybe I am. Because disabled people have no choice and they need our helps, but LGTBQ have a choice and they have good limbs. By the way, this kind of discrimination is the most complex; so many reasons why they are being discriminated, depending on whom you talk to. Religious people would say their religion is against homosexuality, homophobes would say they are dirty and dangerous, but most of us probably would say they are strange and not one of us. For sure, LGTBQ are minority groups but they are not strange; their existence is as old as our history. Just because they are different from the heterosexual mainstream shouldn't subject them to discrimination. They should have the freedom as we have, choosing what they want to be, including sexual prefer-ences. If we don't discriminate people who don't eat what we eat or eat what we don't eat, we shouldn't discriminate LGTBQ either. Leave them alone and let them do what they want as long as they don't violate any laws.

Mrs. Faith: Also, you've commented on the new types of public restrooms, which are designed to accommodate transgender, as ridiculous and unnecessary. Would you explain why?

Mr. Lee: Look, I really think it's a dumb idea for so many reasons. Number one: we generally can't tell a transgender unless we are told. So, why we have to worry about they will invade our privacy or we invade theirs? Number two: if a transgender wants to have more privacy he/she can always use a stall instead. Number three: we'll need a lot more restrooms if we replace the traditional men and women restrooms with unisex or all-gender restrooms, or we'll have a long line to wait. Number four: since unisex or all-gender restrooms can be used by both men and women, they tend to be messy and unsanitary because men don't sit down and some inconsiderate women may choose to squat on the seat because its messiness and, therefore, make it messier. Number five: for a very small percentage of minorities and for such a trivial reason, we have to make such a big change and spend an absurd amount of money and inconvenience the rest of the population? This is another manifestation of over-the-board reactions on discrimination issues.

Mrs. Faith: I agree with you. The restroom situation is terrible, long line and messy, especially for us women. But, LGTBQ are minorities too, they should be protected just like other minorities under the law.

Mr. Lee: I have no problem with that. I wish we have more of them.

Mrs. Faith: More of what, restrooms or LGTBQ?

Mr. Lee: LGTBQ.

Mrs. Faith: Why?

Mr. Lee: Why? They'll help us solving the problem of over-population!

Mr. Lee exclaimed, and then he laughed out loud, and the whole room followed including the now noiseless Miss Jones who managed to force a discreet smile.

Chapter 6: Discrimination of Age and Others

Mr. Rosenthal: Mr. Lee, you haven't talk much about age and other discriminations. Have you ever felt you are being discriminated against because of your age?

Mr. Lee: Am I getting to that point already? No. I haven't felt it yet, perhaps I'm still healthy and alert. Actually, there is no such a thing as "age discrimination;" it should be called "senile discrimination," for people don't discriminate you because you are over certain age, but they do when you are senile. Age and senility are two different things; some eighty-year-old like me is not senile, but some fifty-year-old is, depending on their health conditions. Generally, we do treat the young and the old differently though, because the lack of experience of the young and the mental deterioration of the old. It is a natural response for us not to take them seriously because of that. How can we discriminate someone we love and respect? There is no discrimination against age; it is discrimination against disability of performance. For age is an elusive thing; there is no clear line separating the young from the mature and the mature from the old and, therefore, it's difficult to classify people by their age.

Besides age, there are many other forms of discriminations. We discriminate people who have bad manners, who have poor hygiene, who dress distastefully or act weirdly. We discriminate people who have different religion or no religion or come from other country or speak different language. And, the industrious discriminate the lazy; the educated, the illiterates; the rich, the poor. And you may not believe it, even the poor discriminate the rich and the uneducated, the educated. Discrimination is everywhere and will be here to stay because it is in our genes. There is no way to get rid of discrimination because we have no control over others not to discrimi-nate. But, I think most of the discriminations are psycho-logical and self-inflicted. We, especially those who have inferior complex, are too sensitive to what others say or do. If we can just turn down our sensitivity level and not think negatively, discrimination will no longer bother you.

Chapter 7: People Profiling

Since Miss Jones, the activist from Chicago, was practically shut out of the debate – she had once contemplated leaving the room but decided not to, because she knew she would not be invited back next time if she did, and to be invited by a big shot like Mr. Medford was a great honor. The other part-time activist, Mr. Brown, jumped in to take her place. Unlike Miss Jones though, he was a smart man and he understood why she had fallen from grace, and he was not going to follow suit. So he asked Mr. Lee politely.

Mr. Brown: Mr. Lee, sir, in your book you said profiling is not discrimination, but I think it is. Can you tell me why I'm wrong?

Mr. Lee: Of course I can. Once a wise man said, "Nothing is wrong with profiling. It's commonsense, stupid." And I agree with him totally. It is not only commonsense but also necessary in order for us to make a sound decision, such as not going to a neighborhood with high crime profile or not staying out in the street after mid-night, which is considered the most dangerous hours. We profile a country and its people to evaluate if it is safe to travel to or to do business with. We profile a place, a hotel, a restaurant, a bar, a store by their appearances to assess their merits. We profile people by nationality, race, religion, occupation, and social and financial standing to better understand their characters. Banks and businesses profile their customers to determine their credit worthiness. We even profile men, women, and children; we generally are more wary with men than with women and children. In short, we profile everything and everyone, not just minorities, but majority also. So, profiling is not discriminatory, just as classifying is not. On the surface profiling and discrimination are almost synonymous, but they are not; discrimination is a reaction but profiling is a process. While discrimination is mostly used negatively, though it can also be used positively, profiling is more or less neutral. Using profiling in association with race, gender, religion, and ethnic groups, is usually negative; but using it to evaluate our credit ratings, which is based on how well we fulfil our financial obligations, is definitely positive.

Mr. Brown: Now, assuming I am visiting a friend in a White neighborhood and am being profiled by police as a criminal, and they stop-and-frisk me. Does it considered as racial discrimination?

Mr. Lee: I better have Mr. Hill answer your question; he is an expert of law.

Mr. Hill: It is a very good question, Mr. Brown, but a tricky one. My answer is yes and no. I'd say yes if the police officer stops and frisks you solely because you're black or he treats you harshly. No, if he does that because you are acting suspiciously or he treats you civilly. But the problem is that nobody knows for sure which is which except the police officer himself.

Mr. Brown: How can we know our civil right is not violated, Mr. Hill?

Mr. Hill: In such situation, I suggest we should act civilly and give the police officer our full cooperation, and, if he still treats you unfairly, then you know he is a racist. My advice is: always be a civil person first and give others a chance to prove themselves. Anyway, there are laws to protect everyone's civil right, but don't be violent, use the proper channel to voice your grievances. Unfortunately, not many people who are under such stressful a situation can stay cool; they tend to get angry and act violently. I believe profiling is necessary; without it, it is difficult to identify criminals from ordinary law-abiding citizens. And as to using excessive force, I better let Mr. Hernandez tell us something from his many years of experience as a police officer, Mr. Hernandez, do you mind?

Mr. Hernandez: Not at all. You're right, Mr. Hill, if we all behave civilly and nice to each other, a lot of violent incidents can be avoided. Too bad people are getting more violent nowadays, not like before; they disobey orders and fight arrests. When you doing that even a very nice officer will get mad and end up using excessive force. Of course, there are always some bad policemen, just like there are always some bad people in every race, every community, and every country. People don't understand how dangerous our job is. Every time we leave home going to work we feel like going to war and don't know whether we'll come back alive. This is very hard on our family too. Every time we confront a suspect it is a life-or-death situation; you have no idea how nervous we are. We are dealing mostly with criminals, not nice ordinary folks, and they have guns and won't hesitate for a blink to use them. We have to be ready all the time for a shootout because we don't know what he will do. We may get killed any moment and quite a few of us did. The funny thing is: when a cop got killed nobody care, but if it's a minority, it is a big deal. Very unfair!

As to profiling, it's hard not to; we rely heavily on it to catch criminals and keep neighborhoods safe. We tend to treat people as a group, by nationality, race, type and association; just as we treat rattle snakes, crocodiles, and any other dangerous animals as our natural enemies.

Even though some of them wouldn't harm us unless we threaten them, but, would you try to find out which poisonous snake would bite you and which one would kiss you? No, you wouldn't. You would treat them all the *same* – dangerous snakes. I'm a minority and I live and work in minority community all my life and I have no reason to discriminate one of my own, but, I have to profile a person. Be very honest with you, as a person and as a policeman, I'm afraid of a Black man the most, second is a Hispanic man with tattoos on his neck, third is a White man, and fourth is a Middle-Eastern man with a long beard. Funny, Asians and Native Indians are the least I fear. My ranking is strictly based on my own experience and has nothing to do with prejudice because I believe I have none. The reason that I'm not afraid of Asians and Native Indians is because they always obey my orders and never try to fight me or run away, in another word, they cooperate very peacefully—.

Mr. Hill: Thank you very much, Mr. Hernandez. I know it is unfair to make that kind of assumption solely based on the look of a person. Why should a law-abiding citizen be subjected to this kind of treatment? But what other choice do we have? Do you have any suggestions?

Mr. Hernandez: Well, if one can improve one's credit score by paying bills promptly, so can a race improve its profile by committing less crimes and behaving more civilly when confronted by police. The Asians are a good example: they mind their own business and avoid at all cost tangling with the laws, which they consider a great dishonor and a disgrace to their families and a stigma to their race if they do. They care about the reputation of their family names and their race. Too bad other minorities do not do the same. Their parents and civil leaders, instead of guiding and cultivating their people to be law-abiding, industrious citizens, they side with them every time they get into trouble with the law, even they know they are on the *wrong* side. With this kind of close-eyed supports and encouragements, it's no surprise to me that they are getting more and more violent and lawless.

The story of Mr. Hernandez's personal experience, though a little lengthy, had grabbed his audience's attention. They never thought of a cop as a person who is vulnerable to fear and capable to be nervous. They always thought of a cop as a formidable force and a bully, which was the image of what they saw on TV. Now, they understood cops better and had a little more respect for them too.

Mr. Hill: Perhaps, a national I.D. card would be a fair solution. It would help identifying ourselves in case we got stopped and questioned by the police, which should avoid most violent incidents and hostilities toward police. We're already required by law to carry a driver's license when we drive, anyway.
Mr. Brown: I can understand that, Mr. Hill, profiling is a part of life, but sometimes people use profiling to discriminate; for instance, only recently our president called Coronavirus, Chinese virus, and that is a racist remark. No wonder there are a lot of Asians voice their objections.
Mr. Hill: His remark may or may not be racist, only he knows. But using the name of the place where the disease was originated is very common. We have Spanish Flu, Hong Kong Flu, Mexican Swine Flu, and so forth; and nobody made a fuss until we introduced this crazy idea of "political correctness." You know, the few attention-

getters who complained have their own motive and they did a disservice to American people. They stirred up resentments among us. And the Chinese government, too, raised its objection in order to stir up national sentiment against us. Don't forget we have a trade war with them right now. You see, everybody plays the race card to gain something.

Mr. Lee: I want to add something to profiling. The recent Covid-19 pandemic is a good example to demonstrate how people so carelessly overuse "racial discrimination." The pandemic first started in Wuhan, China, where a lot of people have died of it, and because of this, people are suddenly afraid of Asians, thinking we are dangerous. They stare at us and avoid us as if we were lepers. Now, quite a few Asians, some of them are not even Chinese or have ever been to China before, are making loud noises, claiming racial discrimination. I'm a Chinese and I look Asian and I'm aware of people's staring and avoiding, but I don't consider their reactions are racially motivated. It is profiling and discrimination for sure, but it is not racial and it is not malicious. What they are doing is perfectly normal and understandable and I don't blame them at all. If I were them I'll do exactly the same. Recently, my wife and I avoid going grocery shopping at Chinese markets and when we saw or heard some Asian nearby we'd stay away from them. We can't be racists, can we? It is purely commonsense; we don't know if they are not from China and carry the virus. I even warn our Asian friends to be careful these days when going out: avoid coughing and sneezing and keep a good distance from other people and act considerately, because there are more angry and short-fused people out there these days, and it won't take much to make them blowing up.

Chapter 8: Freedom of speech

Mr. Brown had been nodding his head off approvingly while he was listening to Mr. Lee's answer to his questions, not only showing his keen attention but also much appreciation, which made Mr. Lee so happy that he had almost forgotten the unpleasant verbal exchange with Miss Jones a few minutes before. As soon as Mr. Hill and Mr. Lee finished answering his people-profiling questions, he asked another one. This one was about "political correctness." He wanted to know why Mr. Lee in his book said that "political correctness" had done more harms than goods in solving racism.

Mr. Lee: Sometimes, having too much freedom ends up having less. Freedoms for some could be restrictions for others. I'd say the same thing with "freedom of speech." In America we're supposed to be free to express our opinions, to say almost anything we want without having to worry about getting into trouble. But in reality, it seems to me, more than ever before since someone had invented the word "political correctness," our freedom to express ourselves has been severely restricted. A lot of words that was okay to use before now considered offensive and unacceptable by certain race and gender, and we can't tell jokes or make comments without risking being accused of racial or sexual harassment. Recently, even classic books such as *Gone with the Wind* and movies that feature police are subjected to ban, and many statues which are part of our past are torn down or removed. But, on the other hand, it is okay for people to attack public officials (only if they are not minorities) by calling them names, by insulting them on popular TV shows and in social media. Consequently, "political correctness" is correct for some and incorrect for others.

Mr. Brown: But we must stop using those derogative words and remarks toward minorities and certain genders. They are very hurtful and demeaning, you know.

Mr. Lee: I agree. But we should do this for both sides and that's only fair, do you agree? Anyway, I still think we went too far with it. Do you think it is necessary to change addressing a female "Dear Person" instead of "Dear Miss" or "Dear Mrs." just because we are not sure the person we're addressing to is married or not? What's so offensive about if we don't know and address them wrong; ask them if they're married before addressing them? Or change "fireman" to "fireperson" just because there are now some firemen are females? I just don't understand why all of a sudden people are so sensitive about such unimportant things. If a word that describes race and gender is wrong, we may as well get rid of all the old books and movies and redo our language. Let's be sensible, all these, right or wrong, are part of our history; they happened in the past, and we can't and shouldn't change any of them. History is a lesson we should learn from to improve ourselves. By the way, what is considered to be unacceptable today could be acceptable tomorrow or vice versa. It is very subjective, depending on the intention of the giver and the interpretation of the receiver. If a friend or a coworker calls me "stupid Chinaman" in a teasing tone when I do something foolish, I shouldn't get upset or feel racially discriminated because his remark is not malicious. But, if a stranger or someone I don't know well calls me that in a not-so-friendly tone, I'd think he is a racist. It is the receiver's responsibility to make the distinction. Too bad, in this "political correctness" environment, some of us are too sensitive, too insecure that they fail to make the distinction. I remember when I was a boy my father used to call me "dumb boy" quite often; I didn't feel it was offensive. I felt it was very passionate, very loving. Since we have no control of how we are treated, it is up to us to make the difference. If we're confident and sure enough of ourselves, we don't let other people's remarks and opinions bother us. We *ignore* them. To think of it, it's impossible to have no one saying bad things of us, even if we're the nicest person in the world. How can we be peaceful and happy if we *let* a few nasty words get into our head?

Mr. Rosenthal: The problem is that most people think democracy is freedom, and freedom is free to say or do anything they want. They don't know freedom is like a knife, very dangerous. It can be very useful if we use it to cut a piece of meat and it also can be very harmful if we use it to stab a person. So, we must use freedom very carefully like using a knife. Every time before you say something or do something, think not only what you want to say or do but also what other people want you to say or do. You just cannot exercise your individual freedom if it will cause harm to others. During this pandemic crisis, protesters bearing signs and wearing no masks, claim they have the right going to public beaches and parks. It is amazing how selfish and ignorant people are that they never consider their actions would cause other people to contract or even die from the deadly virus. And last year there were thousands of protesters blocking the freeway for hours. I know, they have the right to protest but I don't think they have the right to disrupt other innocent people's life. They should have held their demonstrations in the parks, beaches, or on the shoulders of freeways.

Mr. Brown: Protesters have the right to express their opinions and demand certain actions to rectify their grievances, and they have to do it in a way that would get the attention of the authority and the support of the people.

Mr. Rosenthal: There are many legal and peaceful ways to do this, such as: gathering signatures, writing letters to your congressmen and senators, and using your voting power. Violent and disruptive behavior is not a democratic way of which we all cherish; it is an abuse of freedom and I don't think it'll win the support of most people.

Dr. Cain: Nobody has absolute freedom; public figures, celebrities, religion leaders, and persons of vast influence should have less. They should be more careful of what they say and do because their undue influences on public opinions.

Mrs. Smith: I have a question for Mr. Lee. In your book, Mr. Lee, you are pro-choice and you support strict gun control. Why you are so liberal on these two issues?

Mr. Lee: I'm not a liberal nor am I a conservative; I am who I am, say and do what I think is right, and I don't have to stick with only one party like most people do. I believe women have the *absolute* right to make their own choice; no other people including her husband should be allowed to make it for them. It is their body. If not for politics, abortion wouldn't have become a hot issue. You have to understand, most religions are against abortion and they have powerful influence which no politician can afford to ignore. That explains why most politicians are either against abortion or ambiguous about it, even though they, themselves, approve it. As to gun control it is the same situation. NRA is very powerful politically because the enormous number of members it has. If I were a politician running for some high office I probably would've never dared to openly support gun control. You can see now, politics is a dirty game and politicians are seldom good and honest people. They rarely do things in the interest of common people.

Mr. Lee's candid speech was not totally well received; it was a delightful observation for some but a supercilious criticism for the few politicians in the room. It did not sit particularly well with Mrs. Faith who was tense and restless in her seat, feeling angry and humiliated but managed not showing it.

Chapter 9: Equality

Mr. Hill, the former attorney general who was all this time listening attentively without saying a word, sometimes nodding and sometimes shaking his head. But he did it so subtly that only his neighbors might have noticed it. In a calm voice and an articulate language he changed the topic of the debate.

Mr. Hill: In your book, Mr. Lee, you said we are equal only before the law and then you said our laws and courts are often corrupted. Do you know that we legal professionals are trying our very best every day to carry out our equitable laws to make sure every citizen of this great nation will be treated equally and fairly?
Mr. Lee: I'm sorry if I've offended your profession. Perhaps I shouldn't have used such a strong word as "corrupted," I should've used "under the influence of circumstance." But, what I meant is that we're not born equal; some of us are born into rich families and some into poor ones, some born healthy and some sick, some handsome and some ugly, and some clever and some stupid. But we all have equal opportunities and we are equal before the law if the law is equitable and not corrupted. In reality, unfortunately, due to our ugly human natures, the legislatures who make the laws and the judges, the juries, and the prosecutors, who are supposed to carry out the law, are often under the influence of circumstance for whatever reasons, and they fail at doing their duties.

Mr. Hill thought he knew everything about law that there is to be known, yet he had never heard of the term "under the influence of circumstance."

Mr. Hill: What do you mean under the influence of circumstance?

Mr. Lee: What I meant is that there are so many circumstances that may play a role in influencing the decision-making process of the jury, judge, prosecutor, and also the defender. Whether they are positive or negative influences; they all make it more difficult to have a fair and equitable trial. Let me give you a few examples: the jury, which is selected from ordinary people, tends to be more sentimental than logical. The rich and famous can afford to hire the best lawyers money can buy, and they come as a team of experts who are often outsmart the prosecutors and defenders. For the poor who can't afford to hire a lawyer, the court will appoint public defenders for them; but, usually they're new in the business and don't have enough trial experience and also, because they are paid rather poorly, they have no incentive to fight to win. They are more willing to do plead-bargaining to wrap up the case and move on to another.

Mr. Brown, after having a brief whispering with Miss Jones, raised his hand and held it in the air long enough to get Mr. Medford's attention.

Mr. Medford: Yes, Mr. Brown?

Mr. Brown: What's your opinion on Affirmative Action, Mr. Lee?

Mr. Lee: What's yours, may I ask?

Mr. Brown: Mine? I think it is fair; it'll make the playing field more level. Don't you agree, Mr. Lee?

Mr. Lee: I'm sorry but I've to say I don't. To right what was wrong and to make what was inequitable equitable is fair and a must, but, Affirmative Action is like overbending a crooked iron bar, it will remain crooked, but crooked on the other side. It's a *reversed* discrimination. It rewards mediocre students at the expense of outstanding students. Discrimination is wrong, period, doesn't matter it is against the minority or against the majority. Or, it was in the past or in the present.

Mr. Brown: But, we got to give the underprivileged a chance to catch up. You know, they have many disadvantages competing with the privileged, which are not even their fault.

Mr. Lee: Mr. Brown, both underprivileged and privileged people have their advantages and disadvantages, depending on how you look at it. For underprivileged people, since they are poor and hungry, they have to motivate themselves to work harder in order to get ahead, and pretty soon it becomes a habit for them, which contributes to their successes later. This is their advantage. But, for the privileged people, they have everything they need and their lives are comfortable, so they become complacent and unproductive. This is their disadvantage. Have you ever noticed that most successful people are self-made and most rich kids end up in the shadows of their parents? Now, Mr. Brown, tell me why the underprivileged need special help?

Mr. Brown: So that more minority students can go to college.

Mr. Lee: If a student is not good enough to go to college, then he shouldn't go to college. He should learn a trade. There are many trades you can make a good living with. But, if the student is a college material and can't afford it, then, the college or our government should come to his help.

Mr. Brown: That's not fair.

Mr. Lee: Not fair! Let me tell you something, Mr. Brown, when I was in college I knew some minority students whose families were poor and they went to ghetto high schools, but they got admitted into a top-notched college on scholarship without the help of Affirmative Action which was nonexistent then.

Mr. Brown was speechless; he knew nobody can argue with the fact, so he changed to another topic.

Mr. Brown: What about Reparation?
Mr. Lee: It is a ridiculous idea, pure greed! Slavery happened long time ago and the people who'd done wrong to slaves were slave traders and some slave owners. It has absolutely nothing to do with us and we've never benefited anything from it. I don't think it's fair to ask us to make the reparation payments to those who've suffered from the misery of slavery, much less to those who've never ever suffered from it. By the way, slaves were not the only one who had been exploited and mistreated, so were the Chinese laborers who came to build the railroads, the Japanese laborers toiling in Hawaii sugarcane and pineapple plantations, the Irish, the German and…. What about them, do we have to pay them too?
Mr. Brown: What about the huge gap in wealth disparity between the White and the minority?
Mr. Lee: Which minority you're referring to, Black?
Mr. Brown: Yes.
Mr. Lee: I want you to know that other minorities do not have large gaps as Black people have; in fact, the Asian's average is almost as high as the White's, and should be higher if we don't include those new Asian immigrants who came here penniless. I can tell you why. They work

very hard and save more. They don't blow their money on booze and drugs. More importantly, they are motivated and have a strong desire to succeed, let it be in education, career or business. Please don't get me wrong, I don't mean there are no hard-working, motivated Blacks and no Asian alcoholics and drug addicts. I'm speaking in general terms. In fact, the rate of increase in net worth in recent years is higher for Blacks than for White, second only to Asians, due to increasing number of wealthy Blacks who find their successes in all fields, especially in sports, business, and entertainment. We even had a Black president, not to mention senators and congressmen and mayors. And, most NBA and NFL players are Blacks and they are multi-millionaires if not billionaires. So, how can we justify there are prevailing racism and inequality in this country?

Mrs. Smith was sick and tired of hearing Affirmative Action because it reminded her that her two children couldn't get in the college of their choice because of it. Although she proclaimed a liberal and a Democrat, she actually was a Republican at heart. She could be anything that suits her.

Mrs. Smith: I kind of agree with you, but inequality in this country is prevailing and we need to do something about it, don't we, Mr. Lee?
Mr. Lee: First, we're not alone; there are many countries in the world that have worse inequality records than ours. For them inequality is a fact of life; people don't even have equal opportunity as we do. Birth dictates their whole life.
Mrs. Smith: Since we have no control of our births, we

must at least fight for equal opportunity and equal rights. Don't you think it's reasonable, Mr. Lee?

Mr. Lee: We do have equal opportunity in this country. If you don't seize it, it is your own fault. But we overuse the word "inequality" just as we overuse the word "discrimination" as an excuse for our failures. We blame it on everything but ourselves. Let's take a minute to talk about equal-work-equal-pay. This is a communist idea which has been proven not working because it is not equitable. Doing the same work shouldn't get paid the same; we should get paid by how well we do the work. Pay should be based on performance and productivity, not on how many hours we put in. It is only fair that a productive worker, even though doing the same work, gets higher pay than a nonproductive one. That explains why a good salesperson makes more commissions than an average one, a good manager has promotions more often and more quickly, and a star athlete or a famous entertainer makes millions while the rest of his field barely make a living. How can it be *fair* if a competent employee makes the same amount of money as an incompetent one, and a hard worker, the same amount as a lazy bone? A firewoman who can't climb ladders and too weak to carry a fire hose gets the same pay as her male counterpart? You got to be kidding! I think we should let the market, not the government, determine how much to pay each worker. I'm sure most companies reward those workers that help them make money. If they don't, their productive employees will be lured away to work for other company that does. I don't believe any successful company would *underpay* their valuable employees for that reason.

I think "Equal-job-equal-pay" is a lofty goal but in reality it's practically impossible. Look at the communist countries, such as Russia and China where equal-job-equal-pay has been practiced for decades now and it had failed miserably. Why? Because there are no incentives to work hard and to innovate, as a result, their economies collapsed. Besides, we can't talk about equality just in terms of *materialism*; there are other aspects we have to consider also. A laidback salesman will be just as happy with his smaller commission check if he does not have to hustle so hard. Oh, minimum wage is another bad law, and because of it many not-so-competent workers who want to work can't get a job, yet they could have if there is no minimum wage law. The reason is simple: businessmen are profit oriented and they always evaluate cost vs productivity. No businessman would hire an employee to lose money. You know, a lot of low end jobs that can't afford the minimum wage go to other countries, and because of this millions of healthy and willing-to-work Americans end up on welfare. They lose their self-esteems and our country loses tax revenues.

Mrs. Smith: If we have no minimum wage law, workers will be exploited and will be working like slaves, and the rich will get richer and the poor, poorer.

Mr. Lee: This is a free country; people are free to choose jobs and employers, and employers have to compete for productive employees in order to maximize profits. Free market is the best way to equalize things and it is fair for everyone.

Chapter 10: Immigration and illegal migrants

The ex-governor, Mr. Rosen, whose state had recently a sudden influx of illegal migrants from South America, was not interested in the forever problematic topic of inequality. He had more urgent problems on his hand right now because he was still one of the advisors to the current governor. He needed some inputs from the group.

Mr. Rosen: I'm sure you all aware of that our country is being besieged by illegal migrants, especially here in Southern California. Every day we have thousands of them trying to get in. Washington instructs us to stop them but most Californians want to welcome them for humanitarian reason. Our governor doesn't know who to listen to. To defy Washington is dissenting and to comply is against the will of our constituents. Either way, a lot of people will be unhappy. What a nasty problem. Maybe you ladies and gentlemen have some good ideas to share.

Mr. Hill: We're United States, a united country. We are found on the principle of working together, not against one another. Besides, the Federal Government may sue any state for non-compliance.

Mrs. Faith: We should let them come. They're desperate and poor, risking their lives and traveling thousands of miles to come here. Are we going to watch them going home to die of hunger or facing persecution? And don't forget, our country was built by immigrants and we're all immigrants or descendants of immigrants. We ought to have some feelings for them.

Mr. Hill: Mrs. Faith, they're migrants not immigrants and they come illegally without proper papers. And, there is another problem: if we let some in we must let the rest in, too. Can we let the whole world of them move in with us? It is an invasion!

Mr. Rosen: Mr. Hill is right; they're illegal migrants. Besides, there are so many of them I'm afraid they'll drain our resources and become a huge financial burden.

Mrs. Faith: Come on, Mr. Rosen, California is rich and can easily take care of them. It is our obligation to see these political asylum seekers are well cared for.

Mr. Rosen: Mrs. Faith, most of these migrants is not political asylum seekers; they're people who take advantage of the loopholes in our immigration law.

Mrs. Faith: It is the law, isn't it?

Mr. Rosen: Yes. But it's an outdated one and we need to change it. You were a congresswoman and it was your job to do that, why didn't you? By the way, they aren't all legitimate political asylum seekers, some of them are criminals and drug dealers.

Mrs. Faith: Even if that is true, but they're poor refugees fleeing from hunger and war. As a fellow human being, we ought to help them even if it may cost us a little.

Mr. Rosen: You own a house, Mrs. Faith?

Mrs. Faith: Of course I do! What kind of question is this, totally irrelevant!

Mr. Rosen: How many bedrooms it has and how many people live in it?

Mrs. Faith: Three, only my husband and I. Why you ask these personal questions!

Mr. Rosen: Now, three bedrooms and only two people live in it. You can easily afford to help at least two of the many homeless people we have in this country. They are poorer and more desperate than those illegal migrants and, besides, they are citizens of this country. If you have your eyes open you can find hundreds of them just a few blocks from here.

Mrs. Faith's facial skin was stretching so tightly over her bloated face that she could hardly move her lips. Only after a prolonged breath-stopping silence that she at last uttered out a few feeble words.

Mrs. Faith: This is a personal matter.

The victorious Mr. Rosen was going to exercise his deadly stranglehold on Mrs. Faith to silence her for good when Mr. Medford, as nervous as a gopher prodding its head out of the hole, jumped ahead of him and said as he was pointing a finger at Mr. Lee.

Mr. Medford: Yes, Mr. Lee, you've something to say?

Confusion swept over Mr. Lee's face for a split second, hardly long enough for anyone to notice it. He had not given any signal wishing to speak, for he was utterly absorbed by the verbal fights between Mrs. Faith and Mr. Rosen. But, almost instantly, he understood exactly what Mr. Medford wanted of him, and he was more than happy to comply.

Mr. Lee: Yes, what I want to say is this: both Mrs. Faith and Mr. Rosen have their points; migrants are a tricky problem. On one hand we should welcome them, showing the world what kind of people we are, generous and compassionate; but, on the other hand, we shouldn't do it because there are just too many of them. How many can we take? How generous can we afford? Letting the whole world come? There will be no end to it! Yes, it's terrible! It's cruel! It's downright no heart! I agree with you, Mrs. Faith, but, if we're nice like we're now, we'll invite not only the poor and the desperate but also all the greedy people in the world to come and rob us clean. We all want to be nice and generous to others, but there is a *limit*, even if they were our own citizens. It's so easy to expect others to be kind and generous, but, when it comes out from your own plate, it isn't that easy, is it? Also, it's a lot easier to be compassionate and generous when you have plenty. It's quite reasonable not to expect generosity from someone who is struggling for survival himself. He may still have compassion but surely has *nothing* to be generous about. Mrs. Faith, we must take care of our own people first before we can talk about helping the migrants. Talk is cheap! There are tens of thousands of homeless people in our country; shouldn't they have the priority over migrants from other countries?

By the way, many migrants are greedy people who do not deserve our help. They take advantage of our kindness and generosity; they come here by the thousands; they apply for our welfare benefits, fill up our hospitals and schools, and take our jobs. Even worse, a lot of them are criminals; they steal, rob, murder, and engage in all sorts of criminal activities. Our neighborhoods and cities are no longer safe. I was told so many times and by so many people that pregnant women come over here to deliver babies. What a great deal for them! Their babies are automatic US citizens and they pay nothing to deliver them because our hospitals are required to admit all emergency patients, even they are foreigners and cannot afford to pay. That's our law and unscrupulous people will take advantage of it. More than that, they, as parents of US citizens, can become US citizens themselves later and retire here comfortably on our welfare. I have some friends whose parents are very rich in their own country, but, when they immigrated here they left all their assets behind or transferred them to other people's names so that they could *qualify* for welfare and Medicaid. They got almost a thousand dollars per person per month, plus medical benefits that cover almost everything, and they'd never paid a penny in income tax to this country.

Virtually, Mr. Lee had repeated what he had written in his book that his audience should have read already, but from their surprised facial expressions he knew not many of them had done so, for what he was talking about seemed all new to them. He was not a bit upset but he was amazed how unprepared they were.

Mrs. Chow: If it's the immigrants, legal and illegal, that *drains* us badly years after years, why we are still unable to solve the problems, Mr. Lee?
Mr. Lee: You better ask Mrs. Faith. She is in a better position to answer your question.
Mrs. Faith: No. You should answer her question. Your book provides all the cures for all the ills. I was only a small potato in Congress, powerless.

Mr. Lee, being put on a tiger's back by Mrs. Faith's shrewd evasion, couldn't dismount now; he had to keep on riding whether he liked it or not.

Mr. Lee: All right. The reason is actually quite simple and straight forward, and I believe most of our congressmen and senators are smart enough to know it already, but none of them *dare* to propose it, for they fear of losing their jobs. You see, illegal aliens are a major source of cheap labors in this country and many big businesses depend on them. Working against big businesses and their lobbyists is as sure a suicide as jumping off the Golden Gate Bridge.

Mrs. Faith: Are you suggesting all law makers are corrupted and lobbying is illegal?

Mr. Lee: Oh, no, not at all. Lobbying is not illegal in this country because we've effectively *legalized* corruption in the form of lobbying. Instead of receiving hard cash, politicians receive campaign contributions. You tell me, what's the difference? They're all the same, money, aren't they?

The room fell into silence again. There were a few more politicians in the room besides Mrs. Faith and they all had accepted some sorts of contributions before, and Mr. Lee's forthright remarks had really touched their nerves, but they all managed to conceal their resentments by pretending the stinging remarks were not aim at them.

Mrs. Chow: You still haven't told us how to solve the problem yet, Mr. Lee.

Mr. Lee: I wish I have the solution, but there is no simple answer to such a complicated problem; so many groups with different interests. The big corporations welcome the migrants because of their cheap labors and the religious and the liberals open their arms because of humanitarian or hypocritical reasons. But the conservatives are resentful of their invasions, and I don't blame them. Who would like strangers barging into their homes without being invited, eating their food and sleeping in their beds! And our government officials, afraid of losing their jobs, are either keeping quiet or playing diplomacy around the issues. Either way, open border policy or building an expensive wall along our southern border is not a solution. I do have a suggestion that doesn't cost us much money and manpower to administer: requiring applicants to show "National I.D. Card" when applying for jobs, for medical services, and for welfare benefits. No more *freebies* for people entering our country illegally, period! When there are no more jobs, no more welfare, and no more handouts, then, the illegals will have to leave and go back to where they came from. We shouldn't help people who break our laws and not play by our rules. We only welcome those who come legally and not become a burden of our country.

Mrs. Chow: You don't think building a wall is a good idea?

Mr. Lee: No. I think it is a stupid idea! Whoever came up with the idea must be very dumb and not a good student of history, and he probably has never heard of the Great Wall of China before, which had cost hundreds of years and millions of lives to build, but failed to do what it was supposed to do – keep the northern barbarians out – and now are tragic relics among the rugged mountains. Ours will cost tons of tax payers' money and it won't work. People can climb over it or dig tunnels underneath it.

Mr. Rosenthal, the right-leaning commentator, had been the whole time quietly listening and watching others getting embarrassed by their hastily prepared questions or arguments. He was a conservative man and wouldn't rush to open his mouth unless he was sure it was safe to do so.

Mr. Rosenthal: What about those who determine not to leave, they may steal or rob or get into illegal businesses?

Mr. Lee: When we catch them we aren't going to send them back by airplanes and buses; it costs us too much money and they'll turn around and come back next day, anyway. We'll send them to labor camps working for free to pay back the damages they have done to our country.

Mr. Rosenthal: It sounds like a communist practice!

Mr. Lee: Not all communist practices are bad; actually, some of them are quite good, worth copying.

Mr. Rosenthal: So, we're going to turn our backs on migrants and not helping them at all?

Mr. Lee: No. We should help them as much as we can but not by allowing them to come in freely and disturb our way of life. We'll help them build a better life in their own country or help them to overthrow their own evil government if necessary. Every citizen of any country has the duty to make sure their leaders are doing a good job for the people. If not, they should vote them out of office or start a revolution to get rid of their rogue government. And, for the good of all the people in the world, free countries like ours have the obligation to help them achieve that goal.

Chapter 11: Welfare and Disability

Mrs. Smith: Okay, suppose we get rid of all the illegal aliens, from where can we find the people to work in the fields, in construction, in gardening, in…? There are so many industries that must have them, and without them even just for one day, the whole country will stop functioning.

Mr. Lee: What about all those able but idle people who live a very comfortable and leisurely life on our tax dollars? Can they work instead of spending their time and our money loitering in the parks and beaches and doing drugs and alcohol?

Mrs. Smith: They won't work for minimum wages.

Mr. Lee: Too bad, they have to if we tighten our welfare and unemployment rules. When you want to fix a problem you must fix all the things that cause the problem. It just doesn't work using the bandage approach. Do you know how many people on welfare and disability, Mrs. Smith? Almost half of the population is on some sorts of welfare and millions more on disability. Don't tell me we have no jobs for them and don't tell me all those on disability are truly disabled that they can't do any kind of work at all! Just take a look at other countries around the world, many people, who would have been on welfare or disability if they were here in this country, are leading a normal and productive life; working as clerks, salesmen, store keepers, and you name it. Why? Because their countries are not as rich as ours and don't have as many liberals as we have, who, with their hypocritically warm hearts, ruin rather than help capable people. No one wants to work unless he has to; it is human nature.

Dr. Cain: I'm not against disabled people, look, I'm one of them now. But I think Mr. Lee is right. People abuse our welfare and disability programs. I'd have never thought of that if not for my recent knee surgery. How convenient to have a handicap parking permit; I can park next to the entrance of a store or a restaurant and don't have to walk too far. Then, I discovered it is harder to find a handicap parking space than a regular one. I couldn't believe that many handicaps are out there until after many days of curious observations and had seen many people who parked in handicap spaces were not handicaps at all. They looked and walked like a healthy person but their cars had a handicap parking permit hung on the rear view mirror. Only later I found out that people either use their father's or grandfather's permits, or do not surrender their own when they no long need them, or, for a few cheaters, bribe their doctors to get one. Am I right, Mr. Hernandez?

Mr. Hernandez: Absolutely, Dr. Cain. We are aware of that but very little we can do about it. One time I questioned a young man why he parked his car in a handicap space, and he said, "To pick up my grandfather. He's inside." Then, he went in the restaurant ignoring me. Since the handicap parking permit inside his car was valid, I couldn't have his car towed and I didn't have a whole day waiting for him to come out. But I knew he was lying.

Mr. Lee: You see, even for a small thing like handicap parking permit, just for a little more convenient, people will cheat. You can imagine what people will do for welfare and disability benefits.

Mrs. Faith: No system is perfect; we ought to allow some abuses. It is not fair to make it harder for the needy to receive public assistance just because a few don't play by the rules.

Mr. Lee: In my book I've suggested a social program called Community Health Center which combines all three major services under one roof. It'll provide health care, temporary shelter, and job training. The consolidation not only will cut cost by improving efficiency and eliminating layers and layers of middlemen, such as insurance companies, independent doctors and private hospitals; but also provides a more complete help to get people back on their feet.

Mrs. Faith: I've read that chapter. Your so-called Community Health Center is nothing but a communist prison; no privacy and no freedom.

Mr. Lee: That's not true. Our centers are not prisons, nobody *force* you to stay and nobody *stop* you from leaving either. Be realistic, you lose your rights and dignities every time you ask for help, but you have the freedom of not asking. It's true that our centers won't give you the same level of privacy and comfort as an apartment provided for free under our current welfare systems, but that is intentional. Who'd like to get a job if our centers are as comfortable as their homes? They'd be staying just like they have been staying on welfare now, forever. Remember, the center is intended to help needy people to help *themselves*, not to take care of them for life. It won't have any incentives for them to be lazy and become parasites of our society. Take a look at the current programs, government pays for or subsidizes their rents and gives them food stamps, and with very few loose strings attached, which are largely ignored anyway. As a result, they stay home all day long, sleeping and watching TV and not going out looking for a job; they use the food stamps to buy booze and cigarettes. What our government is doing is not helping people to improve their lives, but to encourage them to stay perpetually on welfare, and not just for one generation but for many generations to come.

Mr. Brown: Yeah, our support to single moms meant well to begin with, but it's widely *abused*. It not only discourages marriage, but also encourages people to stay single and have more children because a single mom with children qualifies for generous financial assistance. The more children a mother has the more money she gets. I know because I'm a social worker, working with welfare recipients on a daily basis. I know many couples with kids, they live together and the men are making good money; but legally they're not married, so the women can collect welfare benefits. Even worse, it creates another generation of irresponsible children. Raising good children is already difficult as it is by a normal couple, let alone by a single mother and without a father, and that's sad, very sad.

Mr. Lee: That's why I think we need to emphasize on training, not just vocational training but also *character* training which, in my opinion, is equally important if not more so. By and large, people who need help are the problems themselves. They're more likely from broken homes where they get no help to prepare them to be responsible citizens. Among their many problems, the most serious are lack of motivation, positive attitude, good manner, discipline, and the willingness to learn and work. Not until we help them to improve in these areas, vocational trainings and other assistances are futile. We, as a society, have the responsibility to give them *a second chance* – to provide the parental guidance, discipline and facilities to help them to change and become productive citizens again.

Chapter 12: Healthcare

Mr. Rosen, the former governor whose office had been tackling the health care problems in his state for years and without success, was eager to move the debate issue to healthcare. He hoped the brainstorming may help finding a solution.

Mr. Rosen: I think it is a brilliant idea, I mean Mr. Lee's center, and it should work very well if we give it a try. When I was the governor we had been working very hard to improve our state's healthcare system, trying to provide better cares at lower cost to our citizens, especially the homeless and the mentally ill. We'd tried to control the escalating cost of health insurance by encouraging more competition. We'd tried to stop the gouging by the pharmaceutical companies and hospitals. We'd tried to catch those Medicare and Medical cheaters. I've to admit, we failed on all fronts. The corrupted systems, the powerful insurance and pharmaceutical companies, and the avarice doctors and immoral patients are just too formidable for us to tackle.

Dr. Cain: Thank you for trying, Governor, I salute you. Most government officials don't even dare to try. Our healthcare system is too defunct and deranged to be fixed; it needs to be torn apart and rebuilt from scratch. I have a friend who has a preexisting condition of high blood pressure and she has a difficult time to find a company that would insure her. And if she can find one at all, the premium would be *prohibitive, a*lmost $1000 a month and she's not that old yet and is in excellent health otherwise. Another friend has the same problem because he had a hip surgery sixteen years ago. He's in excellent health, too. I think Mr. Lee's health center is a better alternative for common folks; they can have good healthcare at no cost. If someone has the money and desires more luxuries and pampering, he can choose going to a *private* hospital instead, and pay for the services either by himself or by his insurance company.

Mr. Hill: It sounds great but how can we pay for the cost of providing healthcare for all the people? It's a huge sum, you know.

Everybody was looking at Mr. Lee and waiting. Their attentions made his lungs swell with tremendous pride, thinking his novel idea must be an excellent one.

Mr. Lee: I'm only a daydreamer, not very good with numbers. It is the budget director's job to figure it out. All I know is that it ought to be a lot cheaper than our current system. Just the saving from eliminating the middlemen, Medicare frauds, lawyers, and other third parties alone is enough to pay for the cost of operating our public facilities many times over.

Mr. Hill: You still need doctors and nurses and staffs at your centers and they cost money.

Mr. Lee: But at a lot lower salaries.

Mr. Hill: Who'd be willing to work at your centers for less while they can have their own private practice or work for other hospitals?

Mr. Lee: Sure, they'll. They won't have enough patients to support their own private practice. Besides, we'll train more doctors and nurses to increase the supply side, and through competition their salaries should come down.

Mr. Hill: How? It's not that easy to get in medical and

nursing schools?

Mr. Lee: By getting rid of the Medical Board which is created and controlled by medical professionals to reduce competition. But this practice has backfired in recent years because those penny-pinching hospitals and clinic owners have found a way around it. They hire oversea doctors and nurses instead at much lower cost, and because of this, the quality of care is much lower too.

Mr. Hill: I don't think the quality of your kind of healthcare will be up to par. Just look at the communist or socialist countries, even though their healthcare is free, the quality is substandard because their doctors and nurses cannot be fired and their salaries are fixed. So, what incentive do they have to work harder and give patients better care?

Mr. Lee: But we're a capitalistic country and we'll run our health centers like private enterprises. If our managers are not doing a good job we'll fire them. Remember, idea is one thing and execution is another.

Mr. Hill: One more question. How about the illegal aliens and tourists, can they be admitted to your centers when they are sick?

Mr. Lee: Yes, for emergency only. People with health insurance should go to private hospitals. We should require proof of health insurance before we issue anyone a visa. Our centers are really part of the welfare system.

Mr. Rosen: But I doubt your idea can materialize under our current political environment. You know, getting rid of insurance companies isn't easy, let alone Medical Board, hospitals and other middlemen. They can be very powerful allies if they are forced to work together.

Mr. Lee: I think so, too, unless we have a very strong and uncorrupted government.

Chapter 13: Drugs and Alcoholism

Mr. Brown: Mr. Lee, in your book you haven't mentioned anything about alcoholism and drug problems, is your Community Health Center going to be a rehabilitation center too?
Mr. Lee: Oh no, those are not health problems. They are behavioral problems. Alcoholics and drug addicts require no medical care; all they need is a strict isolation to keep them away from their sources of supplies and, more importantly, discipline training. I think a labor camp is an appropriate place for them.
Mr. Brown: Wow! Isn't it a bit too much? They get separated from their families and friends just because they've done a little drinking?
Mr. Lee: No, we won't do that. We'll send only those who have broken the law, not the ordinary everyday drinkers. You know, we all drink a little once in a while, and sometimes more than a little when we're either too happy or too sad. Do we want to be thrown into a camp for that? Of course not!

His honest and humorous remarks started a loud laughter in the room and it lasted for quite some time until Mr. Brown asked another question.

Mr. Brown: Do we mix them with the drug traffickers and the illegal migrants?
Mr. Lee: No, we'll send them to a less harsh camp, more aptly called Reform Camp, where they'll be reformed and then released back to the society once their addictions are cured. Only the incorrigibles and repeaters would be kept

there for a long time. As for the drug traffickers and pushers, they'll be working in hard labor camp indefinitely for they are dangerous criminals.

Mr. Brown: What about humanity, Mr. Lee?

Mr. Lee: One-way or two-way?

Mr. Brown: One-way or two-way! You mean humanity has two ways?

Mr. Lee: Mr. Brown, everything has two ways or two sides. One-way humanity is nice to only the good or the bad guys. Two-way humanity is nice to both.

Mr. Brown: Do you—you mind to explain to me again, please, Mr. Lee.

Mr. Brown got even more confused; he scratched his head and asked again. He was not the only one that got confused, everyone, including the cameramen, was confused. They all nodding their heads simultaneously, echoing for a clarification.

Mr. Lee: Now, how can I explain? Okay—say, for example: if we put an incorrigible drug trafficker in prison for just a few years and then release him for good conduct, but after released, he does the same thing again, selling drugs and ruining people's life. This is one-way humanity because we favor only the trafficker but not his victims. Two-way humanity is trying to be fair to both the criminals and their victims by making sure the trafficker does no more harms to society after his release. Unfortunately, we see more one-way humanity nowadays because those human right advocates and good-hearted people are too busy fighting for the rights of criminals that they forget that we, everyday innocent and law-abiding citizens, have the right too.

Mr. Brown: Do you really believe your strict drug policy will solve the drug problem? You know, it is approaching epidemic magnitude, especially the opioid problem. Many people have died and many families ruined because of it. We all feel the horrendous impact it has on our society.

Mr. Lee: No! But I believe we should try. We've been combating this drug problem for decades now and spending an astronomical amount of money and human resources on it, and the problem is getting worse. I know the cause of the problem is not a simple one; some said it's the family, the economy, the divorce, the drug lords, the gangsters, and so on. The list is as long as the homeless tents on the sidewalks of many LA's side streets. I don't know what the *root* of the problem is, but I do know one of the problems with alcoholism and drugs are caused by broken families. They are unhappy people who have no hope and no families to go to for comfort and help and, consequently, they resort getting high to forget their miseries. The only hope we have is to find a practical solution to minimize the damage it costs. Why our drug war failed? Too lenient! Just take a look at how other country deal with it, the more democratic a country, the more drug problem it has. I really think we should adopt the drug policies of those countries that have fewer problems, such as China, Thailand, Singapore, Saudi Arabia, and even Afghanistan. They all have very strict laws and severe punishments for drug offenders – long prison terms for abusers and death sentences for traffickers. Unfortunately, the situation over there is changing fast, too, because of globalization; I predict it won't take long for the Asians countries to have the same problems as we have.

Mrs. Faith: We can't copy their policies. They're for dictators and communists, not for our democratic societies.

The way we're doing now is fine. We've been fighting hard to eliminate the supplies and we've made tremendous progress.

Mr. Lee: Mrs. Faith, how long we've been fighting the drug war? It has been a long time, right? Are we winning the war? No! If we are not we must have taken the wrong approach. I just don't understand why we are so unwise to ignore the basic economic principle: if there's demand, there'll be supply. People will always find a way to make a dollar. When there's no demand, there'll be no supply.

Mrs. Faith: I can tell you, it's tough to control the demand. Don't forget we're a free country; we can't dictate what people want. You want to throw all the people who take a little recreation drugs once in a while into jail like those autocratic countries do? Don't forget we are a democratic country. I still think it's a lot easier and cheaper to wipe out the suppliers. We can kill their crops by spraying herbicides from the air and destroy their drug labs by bombing, just like what we did to the terrorists.

Mr. Lee: We've done that already. How much longer we're going to continue this?

Mr. Brown: Mr. Lee, can you give us a little more details about your solution?

Mr. Lee: First, we must impose heavy penalty for drug traffickers, pushers and abusers. Hard labor without parole for traffickers and pushers, and reform camp or community services for abusers. In either case, their crime must be *publicized*: in internet, in news media, and by sending out notices to their families, their employers, and their communities. Humiliation and disgrace are *effective* deterrence. Secondly, we must educate and inform our citizens the evil of drugs, through media, churches, schools and families. Not until people realize that doing drugs is not glamorous but a self-destructive activity, that our drug problem can be solved. Thirdly, since drug is addictive, relying solely on an individual's willpower to quit isn't enough. We must have medical facilities and professionals to help them kick off their bad habits. I don't believe we can completely solve the problem of alcoholism and drugs though, just like prostitution, gambling, and other illicit professions, they'll always be with us because they're part of us. Anyway, I hope, through education and self-awareness, we'll have the problems under control.

Chapter 14: Terrorism

Mr. Brown: As I see it as a social worker the drug and alcoholic problem is particularly grim in the minority neighborhoods for several reasons. One: high joblessness and plenty of idle hours and the lack of affordable entertainment opportunities. Two: hopelessness and despair and dismal living conditions. Third: low education level, broken families, and complacency of their current situations. Mr. Lee, they need more help than your Community Health Centers can provide.
Mr. Lee: I think that is the job of their community leaders, who should motivate their people to learn more and work harder. This is their own problem and nobody can help them but themselves.

The policeman, Mr. Hernandez, encouraged by the overwhelming approval of his last speech, spoke again.

Mr. Hernandez: The problem of alcoholism and drug addiction affects the abusers and their families only, which is a small percentage of the population. I think right now terrorism is more urgent a problem, it affects every one of us. We can't board a plane without taking off our shoes and going through a full-body scanner like you're *naked*. It's downright humiliating and very harmful to our body, too! Our response to terrorism is a total failure; we're being scared into a state of paranoia and misled to over-reaction. Everything we do is *reactionary* after the fact. We secure our airports because they had hijacked a few planes before, we make passengers take off their shoes because we had found a tiny bomb hiding in a shoe, we allow no bottle water or mouth-wash on plane because we had found a liquid bomb, and more recently we install the controversial full-body scanners because we had been informed that bombs can be implanted into human bodies. All the things we do are exactly what the terrorists want us to do – to scare us to dead, ruin our economy, alienate our unity and make enemies among ourselves. C'mon, use common sense. They have a lot of smart brains, too. Why they have to attack our airports only? Can't they bomb our shopping malls, stadiums, universities, hospitals, theaters and train stations? Can't they set fire on our cities, suburbs, parks and open spaces? Can't they poison our water and food supplies and our air?

Mr. Hernandez stopped his sensational speech abruptly and had a sinking feeling when he saw the unresponsive expressions on his audience's faces. Luckily he was saved from falling all the way to the ground by Mr. Brown's timely remarks.

Mr. Brown: Not all terrorists are from other countries, some of them are home grown. Every day we hear some violent crimes committed – a kid carried a gun to school and killed some classmates, a disgruntled employee killed his boss and fellow coworkers, the other day, a madman stabbed his father and his girlfriend to death, and an angry gunman equipped himself like a Navy Shield went to an elementary school, not only shot his mother but also massacred dozens of kids. How could all these awful things happen?

For a full minute Mr. Brown's lengthy question went unanswered, for nobody knew the answer to such a difficult question. Only it was Mr. Lee who had been very quiet for a while had a sudden urge to speak again.

Mr. Lee: I asked these questions in my book published in 2013 when all these things had not happened yet. But look, they've become everyday events now. The good thing is: we don't have to do anything if we can just sit tight and tend to our own business. I mean don't make enemies. Leave others alone and don't interfere. Let them fight their own wars, let them kill one another; we just sit on a high fence and watch—.

But, when he noticed the sudden change of facial expressions of his audience, he stopped short and felt quite ashamed of himself, for he now realized his boastful statement had cheapened him to the level of a shameless, self-promoting salesman.

Mr. Rosenthal: In the name of democracy, freedom and humanity and individual rights, we help nurturing violence and insanity around the world. Just look at the television, movie and video game industries, they're all about violence and sex and weird stuffs. How can you expect young people growing up to be good and moral citizens if we *expose* them to all these junks?

Mrs. Smith: We've to thank the NRA and our freedom-to-own-gun law for all these tragedies. Without guns nobody can kill that many people at one time, no matter how angry and crazy he is. We should ban guns just like most countries do.

Mr. Rosenthal: Gun is not the problem; we need them to protect ourselves and our family and to hunt.

Mrs. Smith: Do we need to use an automatic rifle and a

handgun with many rounds of ammunition to hunt? We probably need more tragic incidents to make people rethink our *unlimited* freedom. Like everything else, freedom comes with a price. Our freedom to own guns comes with the price of massacre.

Mrs. Faith: I don't think we'll have a strict gun control law anytime soon. NRA is just too powerful and it has most Republicans in its pocket right now. It will take more shootings and more lives before it will happen.

Mr. Frost: Gun control, no matter how strict, can only prevent ordinary people from getting hold of a gun; it won't stop terrorists or real criminals from getting them. According to what I know, foreign terrorist groups do a lot of recruiting in this country. Through the internets they entice our deranged young people with money, sex, adventure, and their ideologies. But, there are new forms of terrorism which are far more dangerous and they are sponsored by hostile foreign governments. One form is to use social media to spread fake news in order to influence public conceptions and opinions; another is to use hacking to steal secret information, technology, and money. But the most formidable and would do serious long-termed harms is the infiltration into our colleges and universities. Those hostile countries sponsor and send their brightest students over to study and, after earning their Ph.Ds. they stay as researchers and professors and using their positions and accessibilities to steal our technology and brainwash our next generation of leaders.

"Wow!" that was the reaction from everyone in the room. They couldn't believe this is true. They've heard about fake news and hackings which are petty crimes by idle individuals and scammers. But sponsored by a foreign government? Unbelievable! However, no one said anything but Mrs. Chow. She had the feeling that the hostile countries Mr. Frost did not mention by name were Russia, China, and North Korea. And, because her Chinese husband was happened to be a professor teaching at a prestigious college here, she felt they were under personal attack.

Mrs. Chow: This is absurd, Mr. Frost, it must be one of the inventions by the Republicans who want to discredit China and, therefore, make up an excuse to restrict their students coming here. You know, we have a nasty trade war going on right now with China.

Mr. Lee: Mrs. Chow, though your husband is a Chinese and you had been living in China for two years, you like most Americans don't understand communist at all. But I do. I was born and growing up there and I saw with my own eyes and heard with my own ears what they did to Chinese people. They are experts in propaganda and spying and masters in human psychology. They rule with iron fists and brutality, and so many things they've done were so horrible that no sensible person would've believed in them. Americans, living in the land of plenty and never have to fight for basic necessities, always take it for granted and measure others by their own moral standards. Wake up, American, open your eyes! This is a different world now; you can't be naïve and ignorant any more unless you want to be swallowed alive! Let me tell you something scarier: they counterfeit our currency, which is worse than a real war.

Another loud "wow!" came from the audience.

Chapter 15: Wars and Peace

Mr. Lee: Oh, talking about wars, they are thousand times worse than terrorism. I don't understand why we've *never* learned our lessons. Just look at the Vietnam War for example, how many lives have been lost and homes destroyed. We were enemies with the Northern Vietnamese, we hated and killed each other; but now, we're friends and trading partners. In human history there were thousands of wars, big and small, like this. Not just between nations and different religions but also among tribes, villages, and families. They seem to be everyday stuffs since the beginning of our civilization or even before that. Now, we are concurrently fighting a *hot war* in Iraq, Syria, and Afghanistan; and a *cold war* with Russia, China, North Korea, Iran, and a handful of other small countries around the world. And, in the Middle East, there have been continuous wars since I can remember. The Arabs are fighting the Israelis, the Islam is against the Judaism, and even Muslims are fighting among themselves. We mankind are so senseless, wasting our lives and energy for what?

Mr. Rosenthal: I think the biggest problem in the Middle East is the religion, there are just too many different kinds of religions in the region and their followers are among the most frenetic. And, for this reason, religion becomes the divider of people, pitching the Arabs against the Israelis, the Muslims, the Christians; and even among the Islamic states, Sunnis are enemies of Shiites, and so on. Another problem is that they all have too good a memory. They *can't* forget. How could they make peace if they keep *digging* up old dirt and hating each other for old

wounds? It's impossible to achieve peace if both sides continue accusing each other for all the wrongs done thousands of years ago. Like a feud between families or between couples, once started, it can't be ended until they *finish off* each other. They should forget old scores and old grudges shake hands and start afresh.
Mr. Lee: Mr. Rosenthal, I know you're a renowned political commentator. Are you a dentist also?
Mr. Rosenthal: No. Why?
Mr. Lee: Because you've indeed got to the vary root of the problem.

Mr. Rosenthal was dumbstruck for a few seconds before he burst out a loud laughter, followed by many even louder ones from others. He did not expect Mr. Lee, a serious-looking old man, would have cracked a silly joke like this during such a serious, televised debate. However, he was very pleased with the praise and he showed it by the pride on his face. For the mean time, Mr. Lee, radiating with pride and satisfaction, waved his hands to quiet down the nearly uncontrollable laughter.

Mr. Lee: I want to add something more about wars though. Men like wars; they always do for all kinds of reasons. But the biggest reason is *greed* which is one of our bad human natures. Ancient wars were fought for territories and dominance just like other animals. Modern wars, besides for precious natural resources and economic benefits, are fought because of other far more shocking and sinister reasons. Very often we use wars to advance our ideologies which are not necessary the ideologies of others, in another word; we are bullying others to believe what we believe and conform them to our ways of doing things. Occasionally, we use wars to dig ourselves out of depression by engaging more people working in production lines to meet the enormous demands of our military needs. The last reason but not the least important is the arms merchants and the weaponry manufacturers – from ammunitions to cruise missiles and uniforms to fighter jets – will be out-of-business if we don't have wars. Major suppliers of arms such as United States, Russia, China, and Israel would cultivate every opportunity to create wars to keep their factories humming and their supreme leaders' and generals' wallets swelling.

Mr. Rosenthal: If what you said is true, we never will have peace then.

Mr. Lee: You may say that unless we can change human nature – getting rid of greed and prejudice and replacing them with love and compassion – and start *loving* one another like friends and neighbors, like fellow passengers on this huge cruise ship, the Earth. Otherwise, there will be no peace, ever!

Chapter 16: Free Trade and Globalization

The grandiose reasoning of Mr. Lee's had not put Mrs. Faith to sleep, it aroused her instead. As a liberal woman, Mrs. Faith, with a progressive mind, a passionate heart, an articulate tongue, an unyielding personality, had all the qualifications to hold a high office. She strongly disagreed with Mr. Lee and argued that wars are not caused by what he had put forward but by worldwide inequality, and she further stressed, with noble tone, that, if we can make all the countries in the world on more or less equal footings economically by adopting Free Trade and Globalization, there should be no more wars.

Most people in the room except Mr. Lee were very much impressed by her argument which seemed very sound from a humanitarian point of view, but they had serious doubt that wars can be avoided because of it. They were all waiting in silence to hear what Mr. Lee have to say. With no hurry, Mr. Lee, enjoying the moment of importance, continued rather deliberately.

Mr. Lee: I'm not sure Free Trade and Globalization will increase or reduce the number of wars, but I'm sure it won't eliminate them totally. Look, we've been free-trading and globalizing for a while now, it seems to me we have more wars since. I can tell you why. The purpose of Free Trade and Globalization is an attempt to equalize the world, to improve the quality of life for people of poorer countries. Instead of outright handouts which are humiliating for the countries on the receiving end, we are helping them to create jobs for their people. But, in reality, not all the poor countries benefits from it, only a few developing countries like China and India and Brazil, which are smarter and ready enough to take advantage of it. These countries grew so fast economically during the last twenty years that they become so rich and powerful. Instead of working hand-in-hand together to make the world a better place to live for all, they're getting ambitious. They start building up their militaries, their spying networks, their industries to develop advanced weaponries; in short, they want to be a super power, *dominating* the world, economically as well as militarily. Unquestionably, if we have more super powers we'll have more conflicts and more chances of having wars.

From humanitarian point of view, I have to agree with you, Mrs. Faith, that Free Trade and Globalization will definitely improve the lives of the poor around the world, but the improvement is not even and fair. While the developing countries, which are well equipped to improve themselves and do not need much outside help, benefit from it hugely, smaller underdeveloped countries like those in Africa and South America that need the most help benefit little.

Mrs. Faith: Why? They are free to compete.

Mr. Lee: You have to understand, those countries are really backward, I mean they don't know how and don't have the ability to compete. Look at Mexico, they're our neighbors and they should have all the advantages to get our factories moving there, right? No. Our factories moved to China, India, and even Vietnam except a few low-tech and labor intensive ones. Why? It's the people! The people of Mexico and other backward countries are not ambitious people and their education level in general is much lower than that of the developing countries and, therefore, their workforce is not skillful enough to work the sophisticated machinery. Who is going to set up factories there where there are no capable workers to run them? The labor cost may be lower but the productivity is lower too.

Miss Jones: Here you go again, making this kind of racist statements. It is an insult to say the people of Mexico, Latin America, and Africa is backward and uneducated and lazy.

Mr. Lee: Young lady, watch your mouth, don't put your filthy words into my mouth.

Mr. Lee was so upset (nothing he hated more than having his words twisted) that he stunned Miss Jones with unforgiving reproach, who felt daze again to realize her combative style that worked so well in where she came from didn't work at all here. But their violations of debate rules – no personal attacks – quickly brought about the debate host's intervention.

Mr. Medford: Please, you two, no personal attacks and no harsh words. Go on with your explanation, Mr. Lee.

Mr. Lee: I'm sorry. What I'm trying to say is that we can't have Free Trade with every country; we must be selective. We should levy tariffs on some but none on the others, depending on their competitiveness. Outsourcing too, we should outsource to some but not to the others. Our government should make the decision on what products we can outsource and to which country. We must not let the corporations make that decision because their interests are for their stockholders and not for national security or the welfare of the people.

Mr. Rosen: I couldn't agree with you more. Look at what we've gotten into now after only a short period of Free

Trade and Globalization; we're much poorer than before. We lost our factories, our researches, our innovations, and our service sectors, too, all because Free Trade and Outsourcing. All we didn't lose are unemployment and people on welfare. More and more factories close up and more people have no jobs. So many college graduates can't find jobs for years, and if they can find one at all it would be a dead-end job which isn't what they are studying for. What a *waste*!

Mrs. Faith: Outsourcing and Free Trade are good for our country in the long run; we're exporting expensive technologies and importing cheap consumer products. We save consumers a lot of money.

Dr. Davis: You got it all wrong, Mrs. Faith. In the short term you are right but in the long term you are dead wrong. You don't understand; we have the edge in technology right now but, after a few years when other countries catch up with us, we won't have that edge any more. Believe me, they will catch up with us or even surpass us because they are not stupid, they'll learn and steal our technologies. We are rich now, but, if we don't have jobs for our workforce we'll be poor very quickly. Can't you see? By that time those countries will export expensive technologies and import cheap consumer goods from us, just the opposite as now.

Mr. Hernandez: No kidding! Our government is that naïve, only knows how to export our jobs and let cheap products all over the world *flooding* our markets?

Mr. Lee: You better believe it. Open your eyes and look at China, in such a short time it became one of the high-tech countries by sending their best students to our best universities, hiring our best engineers and scientists, forming partnerships with the biggest and the most ad-

vanced companies in the world, and luring our best brains
with a pay-package nobody can refuse. The end result is
what we got right now: our technological advantage is
almost gone if not totally gone because we have no factories for us to do our researches. Our military is getting
weaker because we don't have enough budgets for it.
We're heading for bankruptcy because we produce less
and consume more. Our country is in danger because we
have so many jobless, hopeless, restless, angry people,
and they are so divided on poverty and racial lines.

Mr. Medford: according to your book, getting out of
Free Trade, imposing tariff, and bringing back our jobs is
the only hope, isn't it?

Mr. Lee: That's correct.

Mr. Medford: But how?

Mr. Lee: Number one: to impose tariffs and make them
higher on the countries that we have a trade deficit and
where our factories move to. This will reduce cheap im-
ports flooding our country and encourage our factories to
move back. Number two: to reduce all income and capital
gain taxes to stop the outflow of capitals and wealthy individuals. Number three: to raise income tax on incomes
earned overseas and capital gain taxes on foreign invest-
ments to discourage our talented citizens working for other countries and Wall Street investing overseas.

Mr. Medford: These are severe measures; do you think
we need to get to that extreme?

Mr. Lee: We have to if we want to solve the problems.
You see, we not only let our wealthy citizens run away
and highly talented young people work for other countries, but also let our Wall Street firms *run away* with our
money too. All our banks, stock brokers, mutual funds,
hedge funds, private equity firms, venture capitalists, in-

surance companies and many other outfits take our savings, pension funds, IRAs, and insurance premiums overseas, and make loans to or invest directly in foreign companies.

Mr. Medford: What's wrong with that? They make higher return on our money.

Mr. Lee: That's true but when Wall Street takes our money overseas, there'll be no money left for our main streets, our factories, and our infrastructures. That's what happened; we can't get mortgage loans to buy houses, can't get business loans to expand or to replace aging equipment, and our states can't sell bonds to repair our crumpling infrastructure. On the other hand, China and India are suddenly loaded with money, thanks to our purchases of their stocks and real estates and the loans to their businesses, that they become our biggest creditors. Do you know, because the Coronavirus, we've discovered something new (not new actually, we either didn't pay attention to it or chose to ignore it). One of the biggest meat packing companies, Smithfield, recently has a major virus outbreak, and after investigation many of the sick workers are foreigners with temporary working permits, and they work for minimum wages. More shocking is this, the company, which is a huge meat supplier to our grocery chains, had been bought in 2013 by a Chinese company (Chinese government in disguise). I'm sure this is not an isolated case, many other companies, including those in technology, pharmaceutical, metal, automotive, aerospace, and other strategically important industries, had sold to (in whole or partially) or partnered with the Chinese government. Now, because of the Coronavirus crisis, we finally realize that we'd gone too far with Globalization and Outsourcing and had depended too heavily on other governments (friendly or not) for our supply chains that in a crisis like this we found ourselves unprepared and helpless. I hope this is a wakeup call for all the democratic countries in the world: don't be short-sighted and don't be naïve. Trusting and depending on a communist country or any country is self-destructive! A bit of good news though, Great Britain, Germany, and Italy, which had previously contracted a Chinese company to upgrade their ICT infrastructure, had said they're now considering canceling the contract. It is really too bad that it takes a horrible pandemic like this to wake up people.

Before Mr. Lee finished, all eyes were widening, jaws dropping and heads nodding. They've never thought of these things before and they were thoroughly impressed by his insight. Only Mrs. Faith was not convinced.

Mrs. Faith: I can understand not to trust and depend on a communist country, but not any country? Don't we need to work with other countries like we have to work with other people?

Mr. Lee: Mrs. Faith, working with is not the same as trusting and depending on. Yes, we can trust and depend on an individual, but a country is made up with millions of individuals, and the individual who is in charge and to whom you trust and depend on at the time may not be in charge anymore, and his successor may not honor his agreement with you. I don't have to give you examples, you should know. Can you see now how foolish to trust and depend on a country?

Chapter 17: Litigious Country

Dr. Cain: I didn't know our foreign policy is in such a mess and I always thought only our domestic policy is in trouble.

Mrs. Chow: What troubles you're referring to, Dr. Cain?

Dr. Cain: Well, we're getting too democratic; we have too much freedom and allow too many different voices. We can do and say whatever we want, and sue anybody we hate. You know, we've spent a lot of time and money to sue or be sued. Do you agree, Mr. Hill?

Mr. Hill: You're right, Dr. Cain. A lot of cases go through our courts are really unnecessary, wasting time and tax payers' money; they can be settled out-of-court amiably. But, in this country people like to sue; they sue their neighbors for their dogs bark at night, for trees that block their views. They sue restaurants because their coffee are too hot that burn their tongues, sue the city because their children got hurt chasing each other in a city park. However, majority are discrimination cases, racial, sexual, gender, age, you name it.

Dr. Cain: No penalty for people filing false claims?

Mr. Hill: Hardly any because the burden of proof belongs to the accused, and it is difficult to prove in discrimination case. Most times the jury tends to side with the victim (the accuser), unfortunately, lot of times they don't know the victim actually is the accused.

Dr. Cain: How much does it cost to file a lawsuit?

Mr. Hill: Depending on the lawyer and the case. Some lawyers are willing to work on a contingency arrangement because this type of arrangement is potentially profitable. Also, if you cannot afford a lawyer, there are many social services and civil right groups and non-profit organizations that will take your case for free.

Dr. Cain: What's the cost to the accuser should he lose the case?

Mr. Hill: More likely nothing. Case is dismissed and that's all there is to it.

Dr. Cain: Wow, that's why everybody sues. How unfair!

Mr. Brown: It's very fair; otherwise, poor people cannot sue. Is suing right the exclusive privilege for the rich?

Mr. Hill: Of course not! That's why we have other organizations to represent the poor. But people are abusing their privileges and we ought to put a stop to it. For example: a convicted prisoner can sue, claiming he is mistreated because he *thinks*, I emphasize, he thinks the food is not fit for human.

Mr. Brown: But, prisoners should have the right to sue if their complaints have been ignored, otherwise, they can be fed like a dogs. Is it okay?

Mr. Hill: I didn't say they shouldn't have the right. I said we should stop the abuse by reviewing each case before going to court to determine its merit to sue. You know, our courts are overloaded and our tax dollars wasted by many groundless cases.

Dr. Cain: There are two more problems in our legal systems as I see it. One is the jury, as Mr. Lee had said, they are too sentimental to be impartial and they tend to side with the accusers and award them an absurd amount of money. Another problem is that we got too many unscrupulous lawyers; for money they are trigger-happy to encourage people to sue, disregarding the principle of right and wrong. With just one click you'll find thousands names of lawyers specializing in injury, auto accident, malpractice, class action, and workman's compensation lawsuits. I think it is outrageous.

Mr. Hill: People are greedy, that's why. They're the ones that drive up the cost of insurance; they *instigate* lawsuits regardless their merits. Since the cost of defending a case is expensive, most insurance companies prefer to *settle* out-of-court rather than to fight. This kind of practice provides easy money for the lawyers and the unscrupulous individuals, and therefore encourages them to sue more.

Mr. Rosenthal: I agree with Dr. Cain that the *root* of our problems is that we have too many lawyers. They are the one who encourages litigious people to sue for a share of their reward money. Look at the enormous amount of money average people spends on insurance – auto, fire, health, life and all kinds of specialty insurance – it's a lot more than our mortgage payments. But, we *must've* them in case we're getting sued or we'll go broke.

Mr. Rosen: The litigation problem is not limited to the insurance industry; it affects real estate development, infrastructure, business and almost every aspect of our life. The California High Speed Rail is a very good example. It should be a great public project which not only will provide fast transportation and ease traffic jams, but also will help the environment by cutting down airplane and auto emissions of carbon dioxide. It started more than twenty years ago and is already many times over budget and still not yet finished because of the many lawsuits brought by land owners and special interest groups. If this project were in China, it would have been finished within three years. Sometimes an authoritarian country is more efficient than a democratic country like ours. They built the biggest dam in the world and relocated millions of people in less than five years. Can we do it here? No! We're too democratic; have too much freedom, too many rights, too many lobbyists, lawyers, environmentalists, protesters and you name it. It's impossible to build a road without the approvals of dozen of agencies and many years of red tapes or sometimes lawsuits.

Chapter 18: Prisoner and Child Labor

Mr. Brown: We all talk about how bad our legal system is for businesses, developments, and so forth, but we never talk about how bad it is for minorities. We throw a lot of innocent people in jails because of that. Look, a high percentage of prison population is minorities. Is it not an indication of racial discrimination and inequality?

Mr. Hill: Racial discrimination, no! Inequality, yes! I don't mean as a percentage more minorities are criminals. Our judicial system is not discriminatory; we prosecute a person because we have evidence that he has committed a crime, and we imprison him only after we convict him for a crime. It doesn't make any difference what his race and gender is. The reasons, however, that our prisons have more minority prisoners are: first, minorities on average are poorer and have less education and higher unemployment rate. Secondly, under this dismal situation, they are more prone to be alcoholics and drug addicts and gang members, who are more likely to commit domestic violence, prostitution, drug trafficking, thefts, robberies, and even murders. Thirdly, because of their poor financial conditions their living conditions are marginal also – overcrowded, broken homes, crime-infested neighborhoods – a lot of them found staying in prison is more comfortable than at home. So, they don't mind to commit another crime intentionally in order to go back to prison again.

Mr. Brown: Now, I understand why the parolees I work with saying "checking in a hotel" all the time.

Mr. Hill: Why not, they have more luxuries inside a prison than they have at home: like big screen color TV, basketball court, gym, and library. Oh, they have their own room and bed and toilet. Do you think they can have all these at home? They're lucky if they don't have to share a bed with their grandparents. I think, like Mr. Lee said in his book, we should send the criminals to labor camps instead of prisons; make them useful people instead of parasites of the society.

Mrs. Faith: Ours is not a communist country, we respect human dignity and human right; we can't treat our prisoners like slaves. They ought to have freedom just like we have. Our punishment maybe a little too light; but to send a person to hard-labor camp for life for spray-painting a wall, it's too much!

Mr. Hill: All big things start small; today you paint a public wall and tomorrow you bomb a public building. We must teach our citizens to respect the law, just as we teach our children to respect the rule.

Mr. Lee had been quiet for a long time now and he was getting anxious, but he found no suitable topics he could cut in to promote his book and his ideas. Now, since Mr. Hill had mentioned it, he jumped in quickly before this golden opportunity vanished.

Mr. Lee: In communist countries prisoners aren't parasites of the society; they're *contributors*. They work hard to pay off the crimes they have committed. Their prisoners are happier because they're offered the chance to pay back the society – to be good, to be productive and useful again. They're healthier too, physically and mentally, because, like ordinary factory workers, they live a normal life without boredom and fear, and more importantly they have hope. Their prisoners seldom return once they leave the camp. That's why it's so important to have a completely *balanced* prison system; a bandage approach won't work. Their prisons usually located in remote and isolated areas with harsh living conditions; they're equipped with basic necessities but no luxuries. Reeducation of the mind and behavior is equally important as skill training – they teach them to be good and useful citizens. They make their prisons good enough to keep them content and healthy but not too good for them to want to stay or return to. Furthermore, they reward reformed prisoners with shorter prison terms and, once they were freed, guaranteed jobs and unification with their families.

Mrs. Faith: I don't know it's true or not but I heard they kill prisoners for their organs and sell them to people who need a transplant. How awful if it's true.

Mr. Lee: Yes, it's awful but I wouldn't doubt it's true. They won't hesitate to eliminate any person they consider incorrigible. You know, they'd do anything that we as a human being consider immoral and cruel.

Mrs. Faith: I also heard child labor is prevailing in communist countries, is that true?

Mr. Lee: Of course it's true. Not just the communist countries have child labor; most poor countries have that too.

Mrs. Faith: It's an exploitation to make children work; they should be playing and going to school, not working as laborers. How can they study if they work?

Mr. Lee: They can do both. I believe working children are better students; they're more motivated and they don't have time hanging around with one another doing silly things. And don't forget, early American children worked, too; they milked the cows, mowed the lawns, delivered newspapers and did all sorts of household chores. We have child labor law not because child labor is bad but because our country is getting too rich. Other countries are still poor; most families need every pair of hands, including their children's, to help feeding and clothing the families. By the way, the word '*exploitation*' should be erased from our dictionary. It isn't exploitation if one works willingly for money, food, prize or whatsoever, no matter how little they are; It isn't exploitation either if one volunteers to work for nothing. But, it is slavery if one is forced to work regardless how much he gets paid for it. So, boycotting products made by children hurts them rather than protects them – it may drive them into begging, pickpocketing, thievery, or into other more sinister professions, such as child pornography and prostitution.

Chapter 19: Education

Mr. Medford: In my opinion I think our prison problems have a lot to do with our educational systems. How about let's talk about it. Since you're an educator, Mrs. Chow, what do you think? Are we doing a good job?

Mrs. Chow: Hardly. Our schools are broke, there is not enough funding; as a result classrooms are overcrowded and there're not enough computers for every student. How can they learn if you pack them like sardines? And, the morale of teacher is low because they are underpaid and get so many complaints from students and their parents. We should fund schools more money, hire more teachers and pay them more so that they get the respect they deserve.

Miss Jones: The teachers too, they're indifferent to the needs of their students. They don't care if they learn or not as long as they get their paychecks. The people I'm working with told me that their kids are utterly ignored by their teachers at school. They spend most of their time working with a few smart kids who need help the least. And because of this bias, there is a huge gap in grades between minority students and White students.

Mr. Lee: What minority students are you talking about, may I ask, Miss Jones?

Miss Jones: Black student is what I'm talking about.

Mr. Lee: Are the Indian, Japanese, Vietnamese, Chinese, and Korean students not minority?

Miss Jones: Yes, but they are smart kids.

Mr. Lee: Do you mean Black students are not smart? That's a very racist remark. If I say that you'll call me a racist for sure.

Miss Jones: I don't mean our students are not smart. What I mean is that racism and oppression denies them the opportunities to learn to be smart.

Mr. Lee: What about the other minority students, they don't have the same problem?

Miss Jones: Well, somehow, they are being treated much better, and that I don't understand. Perhaps they're born smarter.

Mr. Lee: That's not true. They get better grades doesn't mean they are born smarter or having some sorts of special privileges. They just study harder and have better disciplines. And I'd say, most teachers are good teachers and they treat all their students the same, but, of course, they favor good and well-behaved students more than those who don't want to learn but making troubles. In this, Dr. Cain can tell you more from his many years of teaching experience.

Dr. Cain: My wife and I are teachers all our lives, I can say that much, we *do* care about our students and we want to teach them all we know. But the students themselves don't want to learn, what do you expect us to do? It's the parents' job to motivate and discipline their children, not ours. If you have a chance to visit schools in Asian countries as I have, you'll see their schools are much poorer and their classrooms are a lot more crowded; yet they produce much better students.

Miss Jones: Teachers are supposed not only to teach their students useful skills, but also to motivate and discipline them; that's what we send our children to schools for.

Dr. Cain: That's in the old days when teachers are trusted and respected. Nowadays, they're not being treated that way anymore because they make less money than most parents. All they get are complaints and confrontations if they discipline their students. There is nothing wrong with our schools and universities; each year they help educating thousands of foreign students from other countries. The test score of our students is among the lowest in the world and the reason is that our students are not diligent enough; they waste a lot of time playing.

Miss Jones: That's not fair to say our students are lazy. Those I've worked with are hard workers and they are eager to learn, but they can't catch up and their teachers aren't helping them.

Dr. Cain: Miss Jones, I said over all, not particularly those few you just mentioned. Yes, we do have a problem but the problem is not what you think. The problem is that everybody wants a college degree – the students want it, their parents want them to have it – they mistakenly think they can get a better-paying job if they have it. Even our government wants them to have it, too, by encouraging them to continue on to college with student loans. Now, we have more people with a Bachelor degree or higher than people with only a high school diploma, and many of them have no jobs, or, out of desperation, taking a job which doesn't require a college degree. And yet, they still have student loans in their names. I really believe higher education is not for everyone, most students better off to get a job right after high school, and start making money. Any tradesman, such as plumber, electrician, and even a pool guy can make more money than an average college graduate if he has a job at all. Only students who are bright enough and want to be a professional like medical doctors, lawyers, engineers, accountants, and so on should go to college.

Miss Jones: We think putting our children to college is the best investment we could make for them.

Dr. Cain: No more, time has changed. Now, it's the *worst* investment there is! It is a matter of supply-and-demand; when we have more supplies than demands, the price goes down. We should've more vocational schools, train more young people to be useful workers. But, we can't make the changes unless students and parents are willing to reassess their options, and our leaders in Washington lead us in the right direction.

Mr. Lee had been listening, waiting anxiously for someone to bring up what he had devoted many pages in his book explaining why current education system had failed, but, to his astonishment, nobody mentioned it. Why, nobody had read it? He thought. But, patiently he waited until at the end when the debate host suggested a change of subject.

Mr. Lee: Mr. Medford, since education is a very important subject, I'd like to add a few more things, if I may, before we're moving on to something else.
Mr. Medford: Of course, go ahead.
Mr. Lee: What Mrs. Chow, Miss Jones and Dr. Cain were talking about was in theory only, devoid of real life situations, which, in my opinion, is far more important. In this case and for the sake of demonstration, I'm going to use a real story of myself as an example, just to demonstrate to you that self-motivation is the key to success, not only in education but also in career and business. But first, I want to ask Mrs. Chow a question: When you were in China had you visited a rural school house or an ordinary people's home?
Mrs. Chow: No, I had not.
Mr. Lee: I thought so. You see, you're a rich American

exchange student and all your friends there were well-to-do upper class people and you have no need to socialize with poor people. Now, how could you complain our schools are too poor and classrooms too crowded? Since you don't know because you never set foot in any of those places in other countries, I'm going to tell you. They are a lot crowded compared to our standard, average about 40 students per class, and two students share a wooden desk and a bench. At home, a whole family living in a pigeon hole of less than 300 square feet, and the dining table is doubled as a desk where children doing their homework, and sometimes tripled as a bed too. How do I know? That was how I grew up in Hong Kong.

Now, let me response to Miss Jones complain about indifferent teachers. Before I do I want to ask you, Miss Jones, how do you teach someone who doesn't want to learn?

Miss Jones: How could I know, I'm not a teacher.

Mr. Lee: Just suppose you were a teacher, okay?

Miss Jones: Well—well, I can't do nothing if—if he doesn't want to learn.

Mr. Lee: Yes, absolutely nothing you can do! But do you know why some student doesn't want to learn? They are lack of motivation. And why they are lack of motivation? It is because they have lousy parents! You know what, we're one of the richest countries in the world, yet our students are among the least in motivation and their test scores are among the lowest. Our students are not the ones to be blamed, nor their teachers, nor the schools, but their parents. It is parents' responsibility to guide and motivate their children. But, it is hard to motivate them if they've got what they wanted. I was always a very motivated student because my parents were dire poor and we hardly had enough to eat, and we had to help doing house works so that our parents could have more time to earn a living. I still remember how our parents had motivated us: They would scold us when they caught us idling, or they would say, "Because all the hard work we've all put in, we're going to have some meat for dinner tonight." Even when we got scolded we never felt resentful, for we saw how hard they worked to raise us and how much they sacrificed for of us to have a better future. They were truly my role models; from them was where I got my tremendous motivation.

Now, let me go back to Mr. Brown's question about Affirmative Action; I've explained why it's not fair but I haven't explained why it is also unnecessary. For that please allow me to use a personal story again to prove my point. I didn't start learning English until I was eleven years old when I escaped from China to Hong Kong. Due to my age I had to start school not from first grade but from fifth grade and that means I got a lot to catch up. Not only had I caught up, I graduated from elementary school near the top of the class. When I came to America in 1969 to study on a one-way ticket and with barely enough money to pay for one semester's tuition fees and buy textbooks, I knew I must have a job pretty quick. I got one the very next day by calling all the Chinese restaurants near Cal-state-Long Beach if they could use a dishwasher. I started working that night at minimum wage plus free dinner. It was not much but sufficient to pay for all my expenses and I was happy. I had been sleeping on the floor of a Chinese friend's apartment for more than two months until I'd saved enough money for a deposit for a studio apartment in not-so-desirable neighborhood. With sheer motivated devotion I managed to graduate in three years, all A but one B, and got a MBA in one year from University of Illinois.

Anyone should be proud of this kind of accomplishment, but I'm prouder because I did it all by myself. I didn't ask anyone for help, I didn't need Affirmative Action to help me getting into college, I didn't complain and cry out loud, "I'm a minority, I'm an underprivileged, and I'm entitled to this and to that." Most importantly, I never felt I should demand anything from anyone but myself. I'd have been ashamed of myself if I ever did.

Mr. Lee's emotional speech quieted the whole room. From his facial expression nobody could tell if he was proud of his own accomplishments or was saddened by the recounts of his past struggles. Nevertheless, none of them doubted that he was not telling the truth, and they all looked at him with sympathy and admiration.

Chapter 20: Campaign and Election

Mrs. Smith: You may forget our leaders. They are always leading us in the wrong direction.

Mr. Medford: Oh, this year is the election year; it will be very interesting to see how it pans out. But, Ladies and Gentlemen, let's not discussing political issues here, they're too hot and too easy for us getting too excited with each other. However, we can talk about the way our politicians conduct their campaigns and we elect our leaders. In my opinion, I think they spend way too much time and money on campaigning; the money can be put into better use.

Mr. Brown: Not only that, it's not very fair; the rich has a huge advantage over the poor. And because this, all our leaders are either very rich themselves or have very rich backers, which lead to corruption. Why anyone wants to spend millions of dollars backing a candidate? The answer is clear: to profit from favoritism. The amount of money they raise and spend on campaigns is ridiculously huge. It could be better used on cleaning up our cities, helping the homeless, and improving our aging and crumbling infrastructures. Also, the amount of time they spend on doing it is incredible too – they spend more time campaigning than running their offices. And we, the taxpayers, are footing the bills.

Mrs. Faith: Not all politicians are rich or crooks. We invest our time and effort in helping people just like you, Mr. Brown, and in return they elect us to higher office so that we can help more people.

Dr. Cain: Most politicians are phonies; they never talk from their hearts, they're trained that way. They say what people want to hear. Don't forget, they want our *votes*! Do you really think they want to serve us? They want to serve themselves. We just can't judge a person by the way he talks or looks. Even with people we've known for a long time, we still misjudge them all the time. All of us can be a good guy or a bad guy, depending on our moods and the situations. In my opinion, debates and campaigns are waste of time and money. A typical politician has three mouths – the good, the bad and the big – the good mouth says all the good things about him; the bad mouth says all the bad things about his opponents; and the big mouth he uses the most, to brag all the way to Washington. When they're on the campaign trails or in debates, they bull and promise this and that; but once they're elected, they're either forgetful or unable to fulfill their promises.

Mrs. Faith: Most of us try to keep our campaign promises, but, after we're in the office, we realize we have to fight with other politicians who have their ideas and interests. To reaching a consensus compromise is not always easy, you know.

Mrs. Smith: Our leaders should work together and put the interest of the country first and not their own or those of their sponsors.

Dr. Cain: To be fair, we can't blame it all on the politician; we're just as phony and hypocritical as they are. We're all *selfish*; all we care is ourselves. Be honest, how many people really vote for the interest of our country and not our own interest? My guess is *none*, including myself if you want to know the truth. Another thing, which I think is very wrong, is that we vote for or against a candidate solely based on how we like him personally, not his ideas, not his policies, and not his track records. How many of us really know a candidate personally? We know him through the news media, which could project a totally different image of him, depending on how well and how much that particular media like him or dislike him.

Mr. Rosenthal: Another problem is that we're so divided along the party line that most of us vote for our own party candidates without considering their merits and without taking a look at other parties' candidates. I'm sure there are some qualified candidates outside the two parties. This kind of "blind voting" mentality is dangerous, prone to manipulation and corruption.

Dr. Cain: Do you have any suggestion to fix the problem, Mr. Rosenthal?

Mr. Rosenthal: No. I wish I have. I'm a complainer, not a problem solver.

All of a sudden, they all were as silent as a mute because what they'd just heard was *all true* – the rich vote for whoever that'll cut their taxes or benefit their businesses and the poor vote for whoever that'll give them more financial assistance. And the old, the young, the women, the gays and lesbians, the Jews, the Arabs and you name it, all vote for the one they think will benefit them the most.

Chapter 21: Lobbying and Corruption

Mr. Lee: you like it or not, that's human nature and we can't help it. But the lobbying and corruption is a different matter. We really should outlaw lobbying which is a disguised corruption, and it is indisputably a very bad thing for any country. We don't have to look too far, just look at our southern neighbor. With its hardworking people and abundant of nature resources Mexico should have been as prosperous as ours. Yet, it remains one of the poorest countries in the world just because corruption there was rampant for decades.

Mr. Rosen: Well, without lobbying how can we send our messages to lawmakers? How can we change the outdated laws to reflect the opinions of the people?

Mr. Lee: By our volts. If our lawmakers and bureaucrats do not do a good job in representing us, volt them out, just as simple as that. By the way, lobbyists represent the special interest groups, not the general public, and because of this where the corruption comes in. It's a very lucrative business; a lot of ex-politicians turn lobbyists to capitalize on their connections to high offices, making millions.

Mrs. Smith: It's shameful but it's true. Gun lobbying is a good example. Why stricter gun-control laws failed to pass repeatedly? It is because the well-connected lobbyists hired by the rich and powerful gun manufacturers and merchants, corrupt our leaders in Washington.

Mrs. Faith: That's not true! We can't be bought.

Mrs. Smith: Maybe not you, but their campaign contributions and votes are very tempting and, besides, running a campaign cost plenty of money and very few candidates can afford or are willing to pay for it by themselves.

Mrs. Faith: That's why we need the lobbyists to tell us what their clients want, and their campaign contributions help us lawmakers to fight for their rights. Listening to their requests and accepting their contributions should not be construed as accepting a bribe, because we, ourselves only, make the decision for whom and for what we're fighting.

Mr. Lee: The line between a contribution and a bribe is murky and thin. It all depends on the intention and whether there is a motive or a string attached, of which it is even harder to prove. The only reliable way we can tell is to rely on a candidate's track records, which requires close examination. I strongly suggest the elimination of nationwide campaigns, which are money and time consuming, except those grass root campaigns at local level; but to have more public debates for all candidates to participate and give them the opportunities to reveal their true personalities, ideas, and policies. In this way, without the distortions by the media, voters would have much better, impartial information about a candidate. Oh, we should forbid candidates advertise themselves on any form of media, either praising themselves or attacking their opponents, just like we should have with doctors, lawyers, and drugs, for they can easily distort the truth and mislead the general public. The only beneficiaries are media companies and they are usually owned by very rich individuals who, through them, may have huge influence on public opinions.

Chapter 22: Climate Change and Environment

After glancing at his wristwatch, Mr. Medford made a suggestion to move on to other subjects, for the time is running short and there were still a few more topics he would like to discuss.

Mr. Medford: Now, let's spend some time on climate change. It's such an important and controversial topic and it affects all the people in the world. Mr. Lee, I would like to start with you first since you've pointed out a lot of problems but offered no answers.

Mr. Lee: I have a few questions that I want everyone here to think about. First, is climate change a real problem that we have to worry about? Our planet and even the universe have been changing for millions of years and still changing. Remember Ice Ages when the Earth was covered with ice? When the ice melted and became water, it created rivers, canyons, lakes, seas, hills, mountains, and lowlands that we have now. So, what's the big deal that the remaining ice (glaciers) melts? Second question: how can we reduce pollution with so many countries, all have their own priorities, sharing the same Earth? Third question: with billions of people in the world, how can we work together to protect the earth we share? Last question: how can we make people not to harm our environment by producing harmful products, by farming and raising cattle and poultry unnaturally, and by over hunting and fishing?

Mr. Medford: I would like to have the environmental expert, Dr. Davis, to answer these questions first. He has been working on this subject for more than ten years. Do you mind giving us your expert opinion?

Dr. Davis: These are tough questions but I'll try my best. To answer your first question, Mr. Lee, climate change is a serious problem; the pace of glaciers melting is getting alarmingly fast in the wake of global warming which in turn is caused by the depletion of stratosphere ozone. If the trend continues many cities and much farmland will be underwater and many parts of the world will be too hot to inhabit. To answer your second question: very difficult if not impossible unless we get to the point that we either dead or alive. The same thing applies to your third. The last question is easier: stricter rules and laws by the governments if every country in the world participates.

Dr. Cain: As I see it, all these problems can be solve just like that (he snapped his fingers), if we can convince every one of us to do the right thing and understand that protecting our environment is a matter of life-or-death. But that entails us to change our way and attitude of doing things. Many people including well-educated, diehard environmentalist like my daughter, though would painstakingly save used batteries to take them to a special recycling center for recycling, would routinely drive fifty miles or more to meet friends for dinners, flying thousands of miles away for family vacations, and buying all kinds of plastic toys and unneeded shoes and clothes for her children, just for fashion's sake. Why people doing all these unconscionable things that contribute to most of our environmental problems is beyond me. They don't know cars and airplanes burn a lot of fossil fuels, toys and shoes and clothes take a lot of energy to make, and plastic is the number one enemy of environment because it is non-degradable and loaded with harmful chemicals? I really believe we need to work on people instead of working on all the bandaging solutions. Only when people cut down on materialistic consumption and stop using chemicals to produce our foods, then we can save our environment.

Dr. Davis: What you're saying is easy to do in theory, Dr. Cain, but in practicality it's almost impossible, for every country and every one of us has different priorities. In our profession, we understand that survival always takes precedence to protecting the environment, and that's why we are working on all fronts, hopefully, by improving on every aspects of contributing factors we can slow down the climate change to an acceptable level.

Dr. Cain: As I understand most of the world pollution is generated by the developing countries. Are you currently working with them on this?

Dr. Davis: Yes, we are. By the way, they are not the biggest polluters, we developed countries are. They are just doing the catch up, but don't have the money and resources to improve their outdated factories. As I said survival is paramount to these countries.

Dr. Cain: I didn't know that we're the culprit of the problem. I guess we consume so much that their factories bellowing out smokes to meet our demands.

Dr. Davis: That's right. If we consume less, the whole world will be much cleaner.

The whole room was quiet and everyone looked dejected. They hung their heads, staring at the empty space in front of them and feeling guilty.

Chapter 23: Vanity and Materialism

Mrs. Chow: To ask people to give up materialistic grati-
fication and to stop using chemicals in foods, you may
better off asking beggar to give you money. Nowadays,
people worship celebrities and royalties and the rich and
famous. They would spend hours waiting on the sidewalks just to have a glimpse of them. They would spend
big money, even borrowed money, on hair styles and a
pair of wear-and-tear jeans so that they might look like
their idols. They would endure financial and bodily pains
to have tattoos all over their bodies just to be trendy as
those preposterous characters. And, more pitifully, they
would try to mimic the way their role models talk and
walk. People are just crazy for these vanity and materialistic stuffs, which won't do them any good.
Dr. Cain: Worse than that, they waste a lot of time which
they can use for studying or learning a trade for a better
future. Instead, they play with their smart phones all day
and all night gossiping, texting or wasting time on video
games. And, they seldom converse with their parents and
even less eat with them, and if they do once in a while
they look at their phones more than their parents. Same
thing with friends, they would have lunch together but at
the table nobody talk to each other. Everybody is so busy
with their own phone. Why, that I don't understand!
Mrs. Chow: They glue their eyes on the phone while they
are walking too, even when they are crossing streets, ignoring the incoming cars. How dangerous! I can understand that having a smart phone is very convenient and
useful, particularly for businessmen who need to have
constant contact with their offices and customers, but for

students, housewives, kids and the unemployed? I don't get it! What do they have so important that they have to have their phones on all the time?

Miss Jones: They got brainwashed by the media and greedy merchants. It is a scam like drugs. They keep inventing trendy useless things to entice the minority youths so that they can keep them always at the bottom.

Mr. Lee was about to say something not so nice to Miss Jones, but he stopped short when he saw Mr. Medford's warning signal.

Mr. Medford: I agree with you totally, Miss Jones, except that not only the minority youths got brainwashed, all youths got brainwashed, too. Now, I'm afraid we're running out of time and, I'm sorry, we still have one more topic to discuss before I give everyone two minutes to make a closing statement. The last topic is about the deterioration of morality. Who is going to start first?

Chapter 24: Deterioration of Morality

Just like before many raising hands, but Mr. Medford picked Mr. Rosenthal's because it was waving the closest before him.

Mr. Rosenthal: I'm sure you all agree that people are not as moral as before and it is getting worse. It happens not just in this country but all over the world, not just one race but all races, and not just the poor but the rich too. People are getting angry so easily and have zero tolerance and would resort to violence for some trifle matters. When I was a kid I could roam our neighborhood without fear, when I was a teenager I could travel to anywhere by hitchhiking, we never locked our doors, day and night, we left the car keys in the ignitions, and we helped each other even we were strangers. But, we can't do these things any more without getting into big trouble. I don't know why all of a sudden the world becomes so cold and dangerous.

Mr. Lee: I can tell you why: it's because the failure of parenthood and school; they don't teach morality anymore. I know, peer and environmental influence is powerful and unavoidable, but parents and schools, especially the former, should be more influential. If parents guide and mode their children early on by setting a good example, to show them all the good virtues as a human being, to train them the habits of working hard and taking responsibilities, to motivate them to pursue meaningful goals, and, most important of all, to teach them the art of living together in harmony with other people, and to help them to develop a strong character of their own, then, they won't be vulnerable to outside influences. Unfortunately, not many parents can fulfil their responsibilities; either they don't know how important it is of their roles as parents or they just don't care. They let their children grow on their own. We teach children to talk, to use a fork and a knife and to hug; but why don't we teach them all the essential things that will make them a good human being when they grow up?

Mr. Brown: It isn't that easy, Mr. Lee. Most parents are both working, just too busy with their jobs to have time for their children. They drop them off at daycare centers in the morning and pick them up at the end of the day, and then, they have to cook dinners and all the other chores. They are just too tired to do any teaching themselves and they have to rely on daycare centers to do it for them. But, the caretakers are busy too; they have way too many crying, unhappy children to take care of that they get frustrated and angry often. Even the good-hearted and conscientious caretakers cannot offer the children the motherly love they need. It is sad, but it isn't the children's fault or the parents' or even the daycare centers'. The society and the government is the one to be blamed.

Mr. Lee: Wait a minute. Why the society and government have to bear the blames?

Mr. Brown: Well, it is their responsibility to provide better daycare services or to provide enough financial assistance to families with young children so that one of the parents can stay home to take care of their own.

Mr. Lee: Why can't they? No one forces them both to work.

Mr. Brown: Most people need two incomes to survive these days; they have so many expenses, mortgage, insurance, car payments, clothes and so many other things.

Mr. Lee: American parents on the average make a lot

more money than their counterparts of other countries. If they can afford to have one of them staying home, I don't see why we can't do the same. Are we considering ourselves too valuable to stay home and not working?

Mr. Brown: if we do, we have to sacrifice a lot of life enjoyments. We have so many entertainment opportunities that other countries don't have, it is hard to resist the temptations.

Mr. Lee: Now that I understand! Our parents want the best of both worlds; they want children but also want other luxuries too. But, if you're not rich and can't afford to do that; you have to make a choice between children and luxuries. We're lucky that we have options; in the old days before birth control was available people had no option. For the welfare of their children they sacrificed more than luxuries; they worked harder and consumed less, but they took care of their children.

Mr. Brown: But we aren't living in the old days. Life without funs and enjoyments is not worth living.

Mr. Lee: You are not alone, plenty of people think the same way and that's the problem. They think of fun and enjoyment and forget thinking the consequences of their actions. People throw rocks from freeway overpasses at cars below just for fun. They speed in and out of cars in freeways just for fun. And they talk and laugh so loud in restaurants that other folks have to suffer is also for fun.

Mr. Rosenthal: These are minor crimes in comparison with professional crimes. For easy money crooks would fake everything, from as cheap as bottle water to luxury items like gold Rolex watch and Louis Vuitton handbag. Some very bad ones produce fake liquor and wine, health supplement and medicine, even fake baby formula that had killed many infants in China. But the worst and most damaging is the white-collared crimes. Those smart crooks come up with so many ingenious scams that cheat billions of dollars out of ordinary, heedless people and ruin millions of families each year. Wire frauds and phone scams are among the most notorious these days, even governments and big institutions had been victimized.

Dr. Cain: Because the rapid growth of white-color crimes, most business schools now offer classes on ethics, but you know what, they attract very few students. This is a good indication that most young people today care for money more than they care for morality.

Dr. Cain had a lot more to say but he stopped when he saw Mr. Medford taking multiple glances at his watch, which he knew was the signal for him to end his speech.

Chapter 25: Closing Statements

Mr. Medford: Now, it's time for our closing statement. Each of you will have two minutes. I'd like to have Mr. Rosenthal on my right to start first, then Mrs. Smith on my left and so on, all the way down to Mr. Lee at the end. Okay?

Mr. Rosenthal: Thank you, Mr. Medford, for giving me the honor to speak first. I want to thank everyone here for so many good ideas and suggestions, from which I've learned a lot. I'm an old-fashioned type of a guy, getting used to the old ways of doing things and I dislike radical changes. I believe all the problems that we have now is the result of discontent s of those who think they can do better than all the wise men before them. They want to reinvent the wheel. My suggestion is: be patient and make the changes slowly and cautiously.

Mrs. Smith: I've learned a lot today, too, and that's why I like debate; it gives us a chance to exchange ideas and fresh thinking which, I believe, is essential for improvement. When we try to improve on something, we'll always encounter problems, but we'll always find a way to solve them. This process is progressive and we've been doing it from day one, and that explains why we are different from other animals.

Mr. Rosen: The most urgent problem that requires fixing right now is our immigration policy. We must get together to find a common ground to solve the problem. I know it is a nasty problem and nobody really wants to tackle it, but avoiding it is not the solution. The longer we leave it alone the nastier it'll become, and for the meantime we all are getting hurt by it.

Mrs. Faith: We at Congress have tried to fix it every year, but the Republicans time and time again are not co-operating; they've forgotten we all were immigrants once, who helped build this great country, and they now only focus on the short-term negative effect of the poor immigrants have on our country. I realize that there are a few immigrants who are taking advantage of our hospitality but their number is so small that shouldn't be the reason for imposing harsh restrictions on the rest of immigrants.

Mr. Frost: I'm a military man, the only concern that I have is the deterioration of our military; our fleets are outdated and our personnel is outnumbered. We must maintain our dominance otherwise with the rising of China, North Korea and other Arab countries; there will be more conflicts or even more wars.

Mr. Hill: Even though I'm a lawyer myself I think we should overhaul our legal system; it is just too loose and it allows too much individual rights that anyone can sue easily. They not only overload our courts but also cost a lot of our taxpayers' money and raise insurance premiums to consumers. I like to see more strict laws and harsh punishments. Mr. Lee's suggestion of reform and hard labor camps is not a bad idea.

Miss Jones: All I have to say is that most of our problems are the result of inequality and discrimination, particularly in the minority communities of this country. If we can eliminate that we'll have a lot less problems. Stop profiling people by the color of their skins is the first step.

Mr. Brown: I've learned a lot today. Thank you, Mr. Medford, for inviting me and thank everyone here for opening my eyes and ears. Your insights have taught me a valuable lesson: to look at things from different perspectives, which I think, will do me a lot of good.

Mrs. Chow: According to my experience I think our problems and solutions can be found in one place: communication and cultural exchange. If we can communicate with one another better and have no misunderstands, then, we'll reduce the chances of having conflicts. If we can have more cultural exchanges between races and nations, then, we'll respect our differences and start appreciating one another.

Dr. Cain: I'm an optimist and I believe we'll eventually solve what problems we have and overcome what hardships we face. If history is proof, yesterday enemies are today's friends, and old pains are new joys.

Dr. Davis: I wish I can be an optimist like Dr. Cain, but what I see every day is not pretty: the smog in most cities around the world is so thick that people have to wear masks, trash and sewage dumped into our oceans so carelessly that fish becomes inedible. At the rate of our earth is warming up, pretty soon most lands will be either under water or too hot to inhabit. Now, tell me how I can be an optimist!

Mr. Hernandez: I think I can be an optimist; for I believe we'll eventually outlaw guns and people will be less violent if there are enough people die from it. But, for the meantime I pray every time before I go out on duty, and so far, God has been kind to me and my family.

Mr. Lee: I'm neither an optimist nor a pessimist; I'm a realist. I believe all the problems we've discussed today are going to stay unless we can change our innate, faulty natures that make us *ugly humans*. But I doubt all of us can, unfortunately, because we always have some bad apples in our communities, in our countries, and in every race. The only thing we can do is to accept them as an essential part of our life and deal with them as best as we can. But I strongly believe the root of most problems is a small percentage of agitators who capitalize on us silent and tolerant majority to advance their selfish and evil purposes. So, if we, fair and righteous majority, cannot be silent and tolerant no more and decide to unite together to root them out, then most of our problems will be solved. **Mr. Medford:** Well, Ladies and Gentlemen, this should conclude our fruitful debate, and I thank you all very, very much for your participation.

Mr. Medford had successfully ended the two-hour televised debate session, but, to the thirteen debaters and millions of TV viewers around the globe the debate was still on. In fact, it had just begun.